The Secret Language of Angels

What Every Christian
Should Know About
God's Holy Messengers

D1562658

KATHY MURSCH

Hier⊕phant publishing

Cover design by Frame25 Productions
Cover art by Cranach | Shutterstock
Interior Design by Howie Severson / Fortuitous
All Biblical quotes are from the New International Version (NIV), unless otherwise cited.

Hierophant Publishing
8301 Broadway, Suite 219
San Antonio, TX 78209
210-305-5027
www.hierophantpublishing.com

If you are unable to order this book from your local bookseller, you may order directly from the publisher.

Library of Congress Control Number: 2017950639

ISBN: 978-1-938289-62-0
10 9 8 7 6 5 4 3 2 1

Printed on acid-free paper in the United States

To Doug Mursch,

the best brick ever.

Love you so much!

Praise the LORD, you his angels, you mighty ones who do his bidding, who obey his word.

Praise the LORD, all his heavenly hosts, you his servants who do his will.

—Psalm 103:20–21

Table of Contents

Foreword   ix

Introduction: From Angel Skeptic to Angel Believer   xiii

Chapter 1: The Lost Tradition of Angel Messengers   1

Chapter 2: The Languages of the Angels   19

Chapter 3: The Language of Seeing   33

Chapter 4: The Language of Hearing   49

Chapter 5: The Language of Feeling   63

Chapter 6: The Language of Knowing   77

Chapter 7: The Language of Dreams and Visions   91

Chapter 8: Improving the Connection:
             How to Help the Angels Help You   109

Afterword: Guided by Angels in Difficult Times   127

Appendix A: Messages from Angels or the Holy Spirit?   139

Appendix B: Discernment and the One Scary Verse   145

Acknowledgments   153

About the Author   155

Foreword

When I first opened Kathy Mursch's book, I was a little skeptical. The world is full of angel books. Why another one?

As I flipped through, my suspicions only increased. Her advice centered around how to let this seemingly remote, ancient, and in the Christian tradition extremely serious level of reality into one's daily life. Angels, I feel, *are* serious, and books about them need to be serious too. But Kathy's book seemed to be alarmingly full of regular, ordinary, and otherwise everyday situations where she asked for angels' guidance. Were angels—the subjects of Milton's *Paradise Lost* and heavy players in Dante's *Divine Comedy*, not to mention the Bible itself—really served by being brought up in such mundane, non-august situations?

Then I noticed something interesting. Many of Kathy's suggestions about how to connect with angels were backed up with quotes. Settling into the book more seriously, I discovered that, most often, these quotations were from the Bible itself.

Kathy talks about ordinary matters from a perspective that is deeply informed by a life lived within the Christian faith and—most especially—with a deep familiarity with the Bible. That familiarity brought me to a surprising realization: by constantly tying her angelic experiences back to biblical passages, she demonstrates that this remotest and most intimidating of books, composed by countless authors vastly distanced from us both in time and sensibility, is full of examples of straightforward, down-to-earth, and surprisingly often homespun advice from angels.

Angels in the Bible can be terrible in their otherworldly power, but they can also be—it's the only word for it—friendly. They offer advice. They point out simple but easy to forget spiritual facts. They encourage, warn, correct, and just generally *steer* the lives of the Bible's protagonists, helping them to live in ways that are more open to God's presence, more attuned to his wishes, more anchored in the knowledge of his love for humankind.

By the time I got to the afterword, in which Kathy describes how her angelic connections helped her deal with the profound pain associated with the illness and eventual death of her husband, she had brought me around to a surprising realization: angels are remote, serious, and profoundly intimidating beings, but they are also beings who are *here to help us*. By exploring a life informed by a sober, discerning, but deeply open attitude toward the reality of the angelic dimension, *The Secret Language of Angels* shows that when we bracket angels off as intimidating and completely *other*, we deprive ourselves of a gift that, as Kathy points out, the Bible consistently tells us we should take advantage of.

The angelic hierarchies, as described, for example, by Saint Augustine, Dionysius the Areopagite, or Thomas Aquinas, are vast beyond all our imagining, and the beings that dwell there are often beyond our ability to comprehend. But the lowest level of these hierarchies—the level described, I believe, in this book—is filled with beings that were not created to dazzle or terrify, but to assist us in all the situations in our lives Kathy points out, not merely the life-altering or grandiose moments. This unpretentious connection to angels who can help you in any moment is the thinking of thousands of years of Christian tradition, and it is the message of this honest, humble, but profound book.

—Ptolemy Tompkins

Introduction

From Angel Skeptic to Angel Believer

I once saw a bumper sticker that said, "I do what the little voices tell me to do."

"What a moron!" I thought to myself. "What an absolute idiot! I can't believe they delude themselves that way. Voices? That person is crazy!"

Oh was I ever judgmental. I was tremendously annoyed. That particular bumper sticker continued to irritate me for several days even though I never saw it again!

I am a practical woman, an entrepreneur. I like for things to make sense. Voices? No one I knew heard voices. I'd never heard voices. Since I never heard them, I decided that no one else could hear them either. I wasn't quite as bad as Saul persecuting the Christians before his conversion on the road to Damascus, but I was close. I judged people I had never met simply for seeing the world differently than I did.

If that bumper sticker had read "I do what the angels tell me to do," I would have been almost as frustrated. I wasn't just reluctant to consider the possibility that people might be able to hear "voices" or—heaven forbid—they might talk to what they referred to as "angels"; I was dead set against it.

Arthur Schopenhauer, the German philosopher, said, "Every truth passes through three stages before it is recognized. In the first it is ridiculed, in the second it is opposed, in the third it is regarded as self-evident." As far as voices and angels were concerned, it was going to take me quite a while to get to stage three.

My siblings and I grew up in the Presbyterian Church—almost literally. If the church doors were open, we were inside. I was baptized, went to Sunday School, sang in the choir, attended Vacation Bible School, ate at potlucks, participated in Christmas programs, professed my faith in Jesus, and was confirmed.

I grew up, got married, left home, and had two children. Because of the way I had been raised, I made sure that my kids, Bridget and Micah, got a Bible-based education too. We moved several times, and each time I immersed myself in church work.

Apparently there was a huge letter "V" for "volunteer" on my forehead that everyone else could see but me. And let me tell you, I volunteered (or *was* volunteered) for everything.

Sunday School teacher? Check. Running the kids' music program? You bet. Planning the Youth Program? Absolutely. Teaching the Children's Sermon? I was on it. Directing Vacation Bible School? Of course. Thankfully the one thing they never asked me to do was cook. Somehow everyone knew that wasn't my forte.

I rarely used anyone else's lesson plan. I talked to the kids in my classes about what was going on in their lives and what they wanted to learn. Then I would pray and ask for guidance on how to teach whatever it was they wanted to know. I didn't think anything of this at the time, even though it was so contrary to the adverse reaction I had to thinking that anyone was being given direction from an outside source. Only in retrospect can I see what was happening: despite my resistance to the idea, I was getting messages from the angels about how and what to teach. I just didn't know that yet.

After many years working with the children's programs, I "graduated" to adult Sunday School and began singing in the church praise band. Church was always fun and educational for me, but my spiritual learning at that time took place in my brain rather than in my heart. I was definitely more "religious" than "spiritual." I certainly hadn't had a mystical experience or anything. That would have scared me to death.

In 1999 I went through a difficult divorce and remained single for quite a while. This was when I began to develop my angel connection very, very, slowly. I wish I could tell you I welcomed it. In reality, I fought it tooth and nail. During this time I decided to train to become a life coach. As a woman who had taught business seminars across the United States, I thought that coaching class would be a cakewalk. I knew that "pride goes before a fall," but I didn't feel that I was being prideful. I just thought I was extremely confident. I have always been pretty good at intellectual learning, but this particular coaching school was all about living from your heart and I did not have the first idea about how to do that.

The instructors were all excellent, but there was one in particular who had my number. Gina was a smart woman, an amazing life coach, a great instructor, and she saw through me as if I were transparent. It felt like she could spot every flaw within me. It was obvious to her from the moment that we met that I was not living an authentic life, and she was determined to call me on my stuff. Just like a good life coach should, she could see my potential and that I was not fulfilling it.

The "I have it all together" front I projected did nothing for her. She could clearly see that I did not have it put together like I thought I did. Gina not only saw the blocks and the flaws, she also envisioned how fulfilling my life would be if I were true to myself. She saw both the cracks and the potential, and she wasn't afraid to call me out in front of the entire class. Mortified, I considered dropping out, but between being unable to get a refund and *really* wanting the Life Coach certificate, I decided to stick it out despite being miserable.

There were many horrible parts of the training, but one section was the absolute worst. It was the one designed to teach you how to "blurt." Yes, you read that correctly. We were to drop all of our filters and just say whatever came to mind. This was an incredibly difficult concept for me.

I was raised with the saying "If you can't say something nice, don't say anything at all." It was something I took to heart. I certainly never wanted to hurt anyone, so as a child I constructed a multitude of filters between my brain and my mouth—a definite impediment in blurting class.

For the first two days I watched from the sidelines as my classmates spouted off witty and meaningful blurts. I could see them getting more and more excited as they grasped the concept. Blurts filled the air, and I sat in my chair feeling lost and alone. Obviously everyone else in class "got it," but I didn't.

Frustration welled within me. I wasn't used to failing at anything, and I was failing the blurting exercises miserably. As if that weren't enough, I soon came to the horrifying realization that all my frustration and sadness were building up and I was about to cry in a room full of people I barely knew. This was *not* acceptable. I hadn't cried in years. I was a successful, professional woman. I did not cry in public!

Unfortunately there was nothing I could do to stop it. I escaped to the safety of the hall. It was not my proudest moment. Class finally ended, and I went home to lick my wounds.

Some time later I was presented with another opportunity to learn "blurting," and this time the angels didn't let me back out. One day while visiting with a friend,

I could feel something around me, and I got the sense that a "presence" wanted me to say, "*It feels like your life is on fire.*" In my mind that was a stupid thing to voice and I certainly wasn't going to say it. We continued talking. I could still feel this push—"*It feels like your life is on fire.*" "*No!*" I responded silently. I wasn't going to do it. The conversation with my friend continued, and the inner dialogue turned into turmoil. I kept mentally repeating "*No!*" but then would feel even more pressure to say it. Finally, I had to end my internal upheaval. I looked at her, took a deep breath, and apologetically squeaked, "I don't know where this is coming from, and I could be totally wrong, but it feels like your life is on fire."

I couldn't believe what happened next. She was shocked! She said, "How did you know?" Then she proceeded to explain to me that she had been cooking the night before and the food caught on fire and she actually had to call the fire department. She went on to explain that this had also happened before, when, many years ago, she had made an unintentional move and because of this an entire house had burned to the ground. To this day, she still felt guilty.

That, my friends, was my first successful experience with blurting. And though I didn't realize it at the time, it was also my first successful experience delivering a message from the angels. Something changed in me that day, as I realized that a presence outside of me had given me that message for my friend and I wanted to know more.

Then it happened again. I was visiting with another friend when I felt a push to ask, *"What are you running from?"* Inwardly I rolled my eyes. Not again! The pressure to say it continued, and finally the words rolled off my lips. My friend looked at me in amazement. She stood in silence for quite a while, considering her answer. It was obvious that she hadn't realized that she was running from anything until that exact moment. But once she accepted the idea, she broke down and confided in me.

It was my turn to be amazed. Clearly something was going on.

With these experiences fresh in my mind, I headed off to a previously scheduled appointment to get my hair done. My hairdresser Samantha liked angels a lot, and she would talk about them sometimes when I went to see her. Originally, all her talk about angels made me think she was a little weird, but she did a really good job on my hair so I kept going back. Then, in the middle of this appointment she began talking to me about the angels again, and I had a strong feeling that it had been the angels who had sent me these messages.

I was questioning whether or not this could be real or just my imagination. I needed to talk to someone about it, and my best friend Christine seemed like the wise choice. I called her up, but before I could tell her what was going on with me, she started talking about angels! I was floored. This couldn't be a coincidence, but rather the angels trying to identify themselves as the presence providing my instructions.

Believe it or not, while I was opening up to the idea that I might be connecting with angels, I still wasn't 100 percent convinced! I prayed for guidance and wisdom. I had always believed that "hearing voices" was a *bad* thing, not something to be celebrated or cultivated. I wanted to be *sure* that I was talking to angels of light and no one else, so I prayed for "a sign" to confirm I was receiving messages from the angels.

Shortly thereafter, I felt a deep urge to call a business acquaintance I barely knew. This was odd, especially because of our superficial connection. Because of that, I tried to talk myself out of it. "*Nooo!*" I pleaded. After an hour of inner turmoil I finally picked up the phone to call him. I wasn't even sure what I was going to say, but the phone was already ringing so there was no backing out. My doubt vanished the moment he answered the phone. He was thrilled to hear from me and said, "It's amazing that you would call me today. I need a friend. It's the one-year anniversary of my wife's passing." No wonder I had been led to reach out. As it turned out, the exact time of her death was just over an hour before we talked; the same time I had gotten the urge to call. That was the confirmation I needed. After that conversation, I was sure that I was getting messages from the angels.

As another spiritual exercise, I decided to write my life's purpose statement. I sat on my couch and began praying to know and understand my life's purpose. I asked God, Jesus, the Holy Spirit, and the angels to bring me the words I needed. I asked them that if I were really talking to angels, they would make it absolutely clear to me.

After I prayed, I glanced around and saw a piece of paper with the words "environmental healer" written on it and got goose bumps from head to toe! I was excited. The thought of being an environmental healer felt so good. I sat on my couch in awe. I had never experienced goose bumps like that, and somehow I *knew* it was the angels communicating with me again. After several more waves of goose bumps it came to me that I should leave "environmental" out. When I thought about being a "healer," the goose bumps were even more pronounced!

Then the words for my life's purpose statement popped into my head: "I am a healer with the gift of transforming lives." Bingo! The goose bumps were non-stop. I had found my purpose, and I had found my connection with the angels. I could deny it no longer. Angels were real, and they were speaking...*to me*!

This was how I first began working to understand the language of the angels. It is a language I have become fluent in over the years, since I have let go of my resistance around accepting their messages. My work is not about telling you how to think or what to believe. My work is about empowering you to find your own answers with the help of God and His holy angels. Now the angels have asked me to share their language with you so that you can begin to receive your own angelic guidance.

Chapter 1

The Lost Tradition
of Angel Messengers

*For he will command his angels concerning
you to guard you in all your ways.*
—Psalm 91:11

When I tell other Christians that I receive messages from angels, many of them either react with disbelief or think I need psychiatric care. I can understand that, because before I began to receive and understand these messages, I felt the same way. You see, in this day and age, it's been programmed into us that anyone who "hears voices" must be crazy. Some have even expressed concern that I am being corrupted by evil, but a careful reading of the Bible shows us that angels have a long and proud history of helping Christians in need by delivering messages directly from God. In fact, the word *angel* means exactly that: "messenger." As someone who has studied the Bible for many years, it amazes me how many Christians aren't aware of this original meaning.

It's for exactly these reasons that I feel it is incredibly important to begin this book by putting angels and their job as messengers into historical context and to speculate on when and why the positive view of angel communication changed. After this biblical basis is established, the rest of this book will cover the languages angels use to contact us and offer guidance which, in my view, is needed more now than ever.

The tradition of God sending His messengers—His *angels*—to us has been lost and co-opted by more busy-minded, analytical, and "scientific" thinking, but opening ourselves up to Him and His messages and reconnecting with this long-standing Christian tradition give us another way to become active participants in God's plans for us.

In biblical days, if people said they saw an angel or had a vision, no one looked at them like they had three heads. It was more commonly accepted that one might receive a message from an angel of God. For example—depending on which version of the Bible you're reading—in the chapters between the first time angels are mentioned (Genesis 16:7) and the last (Revelation 22:16) the Bible references angels close to three hundred times. *That's a lot!*

These nearly three hundred verses serve as evidence of the many ways angels have appeared in the lives of people in the Bible and will give us a basis for discussing the angel languages as specified in this book as well as the myriad ways that angels serve and guide us. I will be interspersing the rest of this book with many of these references, but here I have chosen several which will show the wide-ranging ways in which angels have interacted with and been helpful to humankind which will give us a good foundation to build on. As the Bible demonstrates, while the word *angel* means "messenger" and that is clearly their primary purpose, they aren't limited to that role. In fact, they are here to help us in a variety of ways. Let's look at what the Bible says (throughout this book we will be referring to the New International Version for verses unless otherwise notated):

Angels are identified specifically as God's messengers.

The angel said to him, "I am Gabriel. I stand in the
presence of God, and I have been sent to speak to
you and to tell you this good news." (Luke 1:19)

This definitive passage in the New Testament clearly shows that angels bring us messages directly from God, as the angel did here for Zechariah.

Angels guard us.

For he will command his angels concerning you
to guard you in all your ways. (Psalm 91:11)

God has *commanded* his angels to *guard* us. This is one of my favorite passages and where we derive the concept of guardian angels.

"'*My God sent his angel, and he shut the mouths of the lions. They have not hurt me, because I was found innocent in his sight. Nor have I ever done any wrong before you, Your Majesty.*'" (Daniel 6:22) As they did for Daniel in the lion's den, angels in the Bible keep humans safe. They do the same thing for us now. The love and protection of the angels is constant.

Angels watch over our children.

See that you do not despise one of these little
ones. For I tell you that their angels in heaven
always see the face of my Father in heaven.
(Matthew 18:10)

What a blessing! As a mom, it's so comforting to me to know that all children have angels to love and protect them. Pope John XXIII said parents "should teach their children that they are never alone, that they have an angel at their side, and show them how to have a trusting conversation with this angel." From the time we are conceived to the time we leave our earthly bodies, we have at least one angel with us.

We are never alone.

Angels make pronouncements.

But the angel said to them, "Do not be afraid.
I bring you good news that will cause great joy
for all the people. Today in the town of David a
Savior has been born to you; he is the Messiah,
the Lord. This will be a sign to you: You will find
a baby wrapped in cloths and lying in a manger."
(Luke 2:10–12)

Most Christians are familiar with the pronouncement that the angel gave to the shepherds after the birth of Jesus. What a glorious pronouncement this angel brought: The Savior was born!

Angels tell us what to say and do.

———————

But the angel of the Lord said to Elijah the Tishbite, "Go up and meet the messengers of the king of Samaria and ask them, 'Is it because there is no God in Israel that you are going off to consult Baal-Zebub, the god of Ekron?'" (2 Kings 1:3)

———————

When we are connected to our angels, we can get messages from them on how to handle life situations—both in what we should say and what we should do. When we follow their advice in these situations, we can trust that whatever comes next is part of God's plan for us, because the guidance comes from a messenger of God.

Angels serve as fellow servants of God.

In the Book of Revelation, John twice falls to his knees to worship an angel, and both times the angel tells him not to:

———————

But he said to me, "Don't do that! I am a fellow servant with you and with your fellow prophets and with all who keep the words of this scroll. Worship God!" (Revelation 22:9)

———————

This passage gives us two important pieces of information. First, we are not to worship angels. God is sovereign and king. As the angel tells John, we are to worship God only. Biblically this is an absolute. This verse also alerts us to the fact that angels are our *fellow servants*, and they do His will as we also strive to do.

Throughout the Bible, the angels also give praise to the Lord, as they are His servants much like we are. By doing so, angels help to remind us of our own glorious connection to God. Angels, who are already so strong and mighty, obey and praise God with all their hearts, as we also do on earth.

Suddenly a great company of the heavenly
host appeared with the angel, praising God and
saying, "Glory to God in the highest heaven, and
on earth peace to those on whom his favor rests."
(Luke 2:13–14)

Angels can pose as humans to bear witness on humanity.

Do not forget to show hospitality to strangers, for
by so doing some people have shown hospitality
to angels without knowing it. (Hebrews 13:2)

We see two angels taking on human form in Genesis prior to the destruction of Sodom and Gomorrah. The two enter town and are greeted by Lot's hospitality even though his neighbors and the others in the city wished to do them harm.

The two angels arrived at Sodom in the evening, and Lot was sitting in the gateway of the city. When he saw them, he got up to meet them and bowed down with his face to the ground. "My lords," he said, "please turn aside to your servant's house. You can wash your feet and spend the night and then go on your way early in the morning." "No," they answered, "we will spend the night in the square." But he insisted so strongly that they did go with him and entered his house. He prepared a meal for them, baking bread without yeast, and they ate. (Genesis 19:1–3)

Because of Lot's hospitality to the angels, his family was allowed to leave the city of Sodom before it was destroyed.

Angels fortify us.

All at once an angel touched him and said, "Get up and eat." He looked around, and there by his head was some bread baked over hot coals, and a

jar of water. He ate and drank and then lay down
again. The angel of the Lord came back a second
time and touched him and said, "Get up and eat,
for the journey is too much for you." So he got up
and ate and drank. Strengthened by that food,
he traveled forty days and forty nights until he
reached Horeb, the mountain of God.
(1 Kings 19:5–8)

Here an angel helps Elijah who is running for his life.
The angel provides him with food and water which
strengthens Elijah to carry on his journey. Angels can
fortify us physically like they do in this passage, but they
can also shore us up emotionally, mentally, and spiritually as well.

Angels speak to us in our dreams.

Twice in Genesis God's angels appear in Jacob's dreams:
first to show Jacob a stairway leading to heaven in use
by heavenly hosts and a second time to reassure him
that he is not alone, that the angel is with him.

He had a dream in which he saw a
stairway resting on the earth, with its top
reaching to heaven, and the angels of God
were ascending and descending on it.
(Genesis 28:12)

Angels perform miracles in the physical world.

After Jesus' resurrection the new church was growing quickly. The Sadducees put the apostles in jail because they were jealous that so many people were turning to Jesus and Christianity was expanding because of their teachings. In this passage, an angel opened the physical doors of the prison cell and brought the prisoners out.

They arrested the apostles and put them in the public jail. But during the night an angel of the Lord opened the doors of the jail and brought them out. "Go, stand in the temple courts," he said, "and tell the people all about this new life."

(Acts 5:18–20)

Angels comfort us in difficult times. Before his crucifixion Jesus prayed at the Mount of Olives. *"'Father, if you are willing, take this cup from me; yet not my will, but yours be done.' An angel from heaven appeared to him and strengthened him."* (Luke 22:42–43) He asked the Lord to take His burden from Him, but was instead bolstered by the appearance of an angel. This shows us that God's will is sovereign and that angels cannot overrule it; however, they are always with us, helping us to have strength and courage in difficult times.

Another example of this is in Acts 27. Paul was a prisoner being sent by ship to his trial in Rome. Hurricane-force winds started blowing, and the ship and its passengers were battered. After many days all on board lost hope of being saved. Paul stood in front of the crew and the other prisoners and told them that God was with them.

————————

Last night an angel of the God to whom
I belong and whom I serve stood beside me and
said, "Do not be afraid, Paul. You must stand trial
before Caesar; and God has graciously given you
the lives of all who sail with you." So keep up
your courage, men, for I have faith in God that it
will happen just as he told me. Nevertheless, we
must run aground on some island.
(Acts 27:23–26)

————————

While not allowed to stop the shipwreck, the angel was able to bring Paul a message of survival and hope.

What Changed?

As these passages demonstrate, it was a common practice for early Christians to rely on angels as the messengers of God—something that I think we should strive to reconnect with in our more modern society. But serving as messengers isn't their only purpose as God's servants. The Bible is packed full of references to angels as helpful and beneficial guardians, protectors, and counselors.

So what happened to us? Over the centuries the Christian community has gone from respecting and accepting angelic connections to thinking that angel communication is at best the product of an overactive imagination or at worst an indication of psychosis or even demonic influence!

While a deep dive into why this might be the case is beyond the scope of this book, I think it is safe to say that one reason for the change correlates to the rise of scientific thought which, while providing us with many, many gifts, has also had some notable drawbacks. The scientific community's admonition that angel communication is "impossible" or "unproven" is one of them.

In addition to the dominance of a more scientific mind-set, there are many other simple and more practical reasons why communicating with angels has fallen by the wayside. Consider, for instance, life in biblical times versus life since the industrial revolution. In ancient times, people lived closer to nature. There were no machines at all, to say nothing of cell phones, social media, e-mail, or the myriad of other distractions that humans face today. Have we become so busy that we've forgotten about angels? In times past, there were more natural pauses worked into the day. People didn't try to fit in a stop at the dry cleaners and the grocery store between work and picking their children up from soccer practice. TVs and radios were not constantly blaring. Back then there was more opportunity for the "still small voice" of God and His holy angels to be heard. There were fewer distractions and more opportunities for silence, pausing, and listening.

No matter the ultimate cause, in my opinion the biggest block to angel communication is our expectations. In ancient times, people believed that angels could and would contact us and be helpful in our times of need, so they were open to the possibility and eagerly invited the angels to bring them assistance. Because we no longer look for signs from the angels, we can't easily see the signals that are there. The Bible is clear that God created angels and has given us access to them so that they can help us in every aspect of our daily lives, but we have turned from embracing their guiding divine presence and many of us have simply closed our minds to it.

Many Christians aren't familiar enough with the angels mentioned in the Bible to even give their names, much less consider them and the legion of unnamed angels as a resource. Try this thought experiment to test your current level of "angel awareness": how many angels can you name?

There are four mentioned by name in the Protestant Bible: Michael, Gabriel, Satan, and Abaddon (one of Satan's fallen angels). Another early Christian text, the apocryphal Book of Tobit, introduces the angel Raphael. Even more angels are named in the Dead Sea Scrolls. While in this book we will only talk about angels from the Protestant Bible, the fact that other texts from the same time period do name more only goes to show that angels are numerous.

As I mentioned earlier, when I tell other Christians about my communication with angels, I typically get one of two responses. First, if the person is a believer in angels or open to such an idea, they almost always ask me to tell them more or even ask me to teach a Sunday School class on angel communication (to which I always say yes!). The second type of response is not nearly as fun: my fellow Christians tend to give me a very skeptical look and quickly change the subject, end the conversation, or pepper me with questions about how I know I'm not talking to Satan. If you too are concerned about the possibility of contact from a negative influence, I completely understand that fear. I used to feel exactly the same way. In the second appendix at the end of this book I will discuss the power of discernment, which helps us answer the question, "How do I know I'm talking to God through an angelic messenger and not *someone else?*"

There is also the stereotype in the modern world that receiving messages from angels is "new age," "woo woo," or just plain "out there." But in my experience, angels give us very practical aid. Their wisdom and guidance aren't esoteric mumbo jumbo about things that don't have any application in your life, though they can sometimes be very deep and spiritually powerful. Instead, angels can guide us in the most basic situations like knowing which job applicant to hire, or in a true life-changing experience, such as putting us in the right place at the right time to witness a true miracle or avoid a life-altering tragedy. But none of this is possible if we dismiss their help and erase their presence in our lives because we think it's "too weird."

It is said that we are guilty of taking Christ out of Christmas, and I often say that we are also guilty of removing the angels from our daily lives. In my experience, angels are available to give us messages 24 hours a day, 365 days a year. Angels love, accept, and want to help every one of us. They stand ready to assist us in our lives, but because we have free will, we need to ask for their assistance. (I'll include a special prayer at the end of this section for that purpose.) Once you ask, get ready to receive! They are standing by waiting for the word that you would like their support.

The other challenge for most people is that, once they've asked for aid, they do not know the languages angels speak and don't pick up on the messages being sent.

The purpose of this book is to help you begin to solve that problem by teaching you the languages that the angels are using so that you may see and understand the signs they are sending. I invite you to say this prayer out loud, asking our Lord to open your heart to hearing the languages of His messengers before we dive into the five languages of the angels in the next chapters.

Prayer

Lord,

You are the great I Am. Thank You that in Your infinite love and wisdom You created angels to help bring me Your holy messages.

I want to hear Your messages, Lord!

Open my heart to learn the languages that Your angels speak.

In the name of Your precious son, Jesus.

Amen.

Chapter 2

The Languages
of the Angels

Speak, Lord, for your servant is listening.

—1 Samuel 3:9

For every one of us, there has been a time in our life where we yearned for spiritual guidance. In these moments, we wish that God would part the clouds and point out the right direction, preferably with a big neon arrow so we can't miss it. Though you may not have seen it at the time, God does provide this guidance—but rather than using neon, He provides help and counsel through His powerful, loving angels. The problem for most of us is that we have no idea how to understand their messages or access their assistance. This is why I truly believe that the best reason to learn about angels is to become closer to God. They are one of the many resources that God has put in place to aid His children in connecting to Him. When you reach out to the full-ness of God's kingdom, it's important to be so in tune with the Holy Spirit that there will be no doubt that you are listening to the voice of God and His loving angels. In this way, you will also develop a personal relation-ship with God which will create a deeper connection to Him. Many people I have talked to have found that their love and praise of God has only grown after invit-ing angels into their lives.

While the angels are always around and with us serving God's will, we generally have a hard time communicating with them. In my experience, it's not because we Christians don't want to connect with them, but more often we simply were never taught *how*.

This is analogous to traveling to a foreign country. For instance, imagine that you are on vacation in a place where the inhabitants speak a language you don't know. During this trip, no matter what experiences you planned with a tour guide or an English-speaking friend or relative, you'd see many wonderful things, but you would always rely on the assistance of someone else to guide you.

But what if you learned to speak the native language for yourself? You could then travel through the country having your own experiences, without needing to have them translated. You would be able to hold conversations with locals, to read the street signs and navigate the cities, and also to easily ask for assistance when you need it. Learning the native language would give you the deepest possible immersion into the culture of that country. We can apply this same principle to learning the languages of the angels so that we can have the deepest possible connection with God through them.

This idea of needing a translator is exactly what I see by and large when it comes to communicating with the angels. Even people who are open to the idea that angels provide guidance to humans often think that communicating with angels takes special gifts that they don't have and they need someone like me to act as a translator. This simply isn't so, and my hope is that as you delve more deeply into the languages of the angels, you will begin to see that this avenue has always been open to you—and to everyone who wants to communicate with their angels. It doesn't take years of schooling or any special gifts; it only takes a willingness to learn the ways that angels communicate. To get away from wanting a translator, we need to learn for ourselves how to speak their language—or, actually, the *five* languages of the angels.

Think of angels as polyglots: they can communicate with us in many different ways. The five angel languages are the Language of Seeing, the Language of Hearing, the Language of Feeling, the Language of Knowing, and finally, the Language of Dreams and Visions.

The first three are based in our human senses. We may see angels in physical forms or in visual signs and cues. We may also hear the voices of angels, as mentioned many times in the Bible. Or we may even simply feel the presence of an angel either as a brush on our shoulder or a pat on the back. Some sensations can also be more emotional or mental impressions rather than purely physical ones. For instance, with the Language of Feeling, you can physically feel an angel touch you, but sometimes you can also have an emotional response—a *feeling*—about the direction you need to go. This can be a little tricky to explain, but these three languages are usually the easiest for us to comprehend since they're based around our human senses, so we will begin our language lessons here.

The Language of Knowing can be a little more esoteric as it doesn't relate directly to a human sense, but rather a strong mental pull, when you simply *know* something to be true even if you don't have any empirical evidence for it. Examples of the Language of Knowing include aha moments or when things that were cloudy or murky can suddenly be seen with great clarity.

The final language we'll cover, the Language of Dreams and Visions, is likely the most controversial of those we'll discuss, but can often be the most helpful. The Language of Dreams and Visions bypasses our thinking mind to allow the angels to deliver God's messages directly to us, either when we're asleep or awake. When these messages are delivered while we're asleep, we say they came to us in a dream—but when they arise while we are awake, it's a vision. The messages and the language itself are the same; the only difference is what state we are in when we experience this communication.

You're likely to find that one language comes more easily to you than others. In my experience, many people just starting to communicate with the angels often find it easier to receive messages through one of the "sense" languages first and then broaden into the other two. If that progression doesn't speak to you, then start wherever you currently feel the strongest connection to your angels. You can always practice with the other languages later! The point here is to go at your own pace and let the angels connect with you in the ways they choose to. Because their guidance is coming from God, who will always know the best way to reach out to you with His blessings and messages, you can trust that whichever language you use first, or most, or feel most comfortable with is exactly how you should be receiving messages. God doesn't make mistakes!

As we travel through the realm of angels, I'll be your tour guide and will teach you how to speak their languages. Once you learn the angels' languages, you will more easily understand the messages they are sending to you. Then you can have your own experiences and receive your own angelic inspiration, without waiting for a translator.

Just as flight attendants make safety announcements before the plane leaves the ground, the angels have asked me to share some general information before we begin on our journey into unlocking a deeper personal connection to the angels:

- While your guardian angel stays with you continually, other angels come and go and are available to assist you with all your life situations.

- Sometimes people ask me if their loved ones in heaven are angels. It's okay to refer to them as such if it's comforting to you, but it's important to know there is a difference between the angels God created and our loved ones on the other side.

- You don't have to "fix" yourself before you can connect with your angels. They are ready and willing to help you regardless of what your life situation is. You are no better or worse than anyone else. You are not more deserving or less deserving than anyone else. Each and every human is equal in the eyes of the angels.

- Your ability to receive help from the angels is only limited by your willingness to ask.

- Asking angels for assistance is never "bothering" or "pestering" them. They don't have anything "better to do." We're not taking them away from a "more important" project. Our angels do not see any of our requests as trivial. Ask and ye shall receive! You can connect with angels yourself. You do not need a doctorate of divinity to do this. You only need to master their languages, which we will work on together.

- The doorway to God and the angelic kingdom is in your heart—not your head. An acceptance of the angelic realm comes through your heart. You cannot think your way into this. Love the Lord with all your heart. Keep the commandments in your heart. Ponder His messages in your heart. The hamster wheel of human thinking will not get you closer to God or the angels.

———————

But Mary treasured up all these things and pondered them in her heart. (Luke 2:19)

Hear, O Israel: The Lord our God, the Lord is one.
Love the Lord your God with all your heart and
with all your soul and with all your strength.
These commandments that I give you today are to
be on your hearts. (Deuteronomy 6:4–6)

- All references to angels in the Bible have tradition-
  ally been in the masculine gender. An example of
  this is *"Then the Lord spoke to the angel, and he
  put his sword back into its sheath."* in 1 Chroni-
  cles 21:27. There is debate as to whether angels are
  male or genderless, and many people have various
  responses. Angels do not procreate so there is no
  need for them to be male or female. For the sake of
  simplicity, I will use the pronoun "he" throughout
  the book when talking about angels.

- Everyone can learn to connect with their angels.
  It's not something you're either born with or not.
  I didn't learn the angel languages until later in life.
  You're never too young or too old to learn the lan-
  guage of the angels. You can do this!

Getting Acquainted with the Angels

The first step on any journey is always the hardest, but
the most important one. The same is true of learning
how to communicate with your angels. The initial step

to taking on any dialogue with your angels or receiving any of their signs is, *always*, to ask for their guidance. As mentioned in the previous chapter, it doesn't matter how much you study any one particular angel language if you don't ask the angels for assistance. They cannot bring you guidance if you do not open yourself to receiving it and invite them to help you in your times of trial.

Before you begin any of the language lessons, I strongly advise you to take a moment to focus your attention on the presence of God around you and to give God and His angels an open invitation to enter your life so that He can show you His path with the help of His divine messengers. I was taught to pray only to God, because of that when I'm communicating with God I'm praying to Him, but when I'm communicating with the angels I'm only talking to them. Some people may feel more comfortable praying to the angels directly, so feel free to adjust the words in any of the prayers throughout this book so they fit your individual beliefs.

If you like, you can use the prayer below as an "icebreaker template" in your conversation with the angels—instead of "Hi, how are you?" try "Dear Lord, thank you for being with me in this and every moment. I welcome and ask for You to send me Your angels with guidance for my life." Mix this prayer up in a way that feels good to you, and expand on anything you would like to ask or tell God and the angels about. You can further elaborate on this to tell them what in particular you feel you need guidance on, but you also don't need to go into specifics if you don't have any or don't know yet what you need. God knows your heart and will speak to it in a way that will be helpful to you in pursuing the path He has laid for you. All you need to do is ask. Then get ready to receive by beefing up your angel communication skills!

One way to deepen your relationship with God and the angels is to connect with your own guardian angel. Making a personal connection with your guardian angel consciously opens your feelings in the same way that making a personal connection to a dear friend creates an intimacy that allows you to share emotions and feelings. Our guardian angels are the ones who are with us through all the trials and tribulations in our lives, and by opening our hearts to them, we allow ourselves to receive their messages through our feelings and emotions.

Like our best friends, our guardian angels are always with us. One of the easiest ways to start fostering your relationship with the angels, and your guardian angel in particular, is to talk to and call on them often, even if you're not expecting an answer. This gives you an opportunity to open a conversation; developing a personal relationship will make it easier for you to hear the messages that they bring to you.

It may help you to increase your intimacy with your guardian angel if you have a name to call him. A friend of mine asked her guardian angel what his name was, and the response she got was "Fred." We thought this was so funny because that wasn't a very angelic or biblical name at all, but the angels explained that they don't care what we call them. They are egoless beings, so one name is as good as another to them. If you want to name your angel to feel more connected with him, feel free to ask him what his name is—but if you get no response, simply take that as a sign that you can use whatever name you like to help you foster a deeper connection. Despite knowing that "Fred" isn't her guardian angel's real name, it's become second nature for Sarah to "ask Fred" or "let me run this by Fred," which feels far more personal and intimate than trying to have a relationship with a distant, unnamed entity.

If you decide that it would be more personal and intimate for you to call your angel by a name—whether a traditional angelic name or something as simple as "Bob"—that can be a good way to foster your relationship and serve as a reminder that you have Bob or Fred on your side whenever you need them. By developing this close and familiar relationship, you open up the doorways of communication and make yourself more available to receive angelic messages.

Then Manoah inquired of the angel of the Lord, "What is your name, so that we may honor you when your word comes true?" He replied, "Why do you ask my name? It is beyond understanding." (Judges 13:17–18)

It can be very helpful to get acquainted with the angels before you delve deeply into their languages, but if you're still having "preflight" jitters, remember that your angels are always on your side; they are rooting for you at every turn and will only ever deliver messages that are in your best interest. While it may seem scary to get started, you are safe in God's hands and with His messengers, whose duties include protecting and nurturing humans with His love and wisdom.

It's time for your angel language lessons to begin! After your lessons are complete, you'll learn how you can use your newfound skills to help you in your everyday life. You'll find that as you become more fluent in the languages of the angels, you will develop a deeper connection to God and find it easier and easier to receive His guidance and to pursue His plan and path by allowing the angels to work in your life.

Prayer

Lord God,

*I'm ready! I want to learn the languages
Your Holy angels speak. I want to receive
Your messages from them. Guide me, bless me
and keep me safe as I begin this journey to
connect more fully with You through
Your loving angels.*

In Jesus' name,

Amen

Chapter 3

The Language of Seeing

*Then an angel of the Lord appeared
to him, standing at the right side of
the altar of incense.*

—Luke 1:11

When I talk to other people about the languages of the angels, they most often wish the angels would communicate with them visually. And why not? Wouldn't it be wonderful to actually see an angel? There is the oft-quoted adage that "seeing is believing," and that's certainly how I felt when I began my angel journey. Fortunately, sight is one of the most common ways angels communicate with us, so we will begin our lessons on the Five Angel Languages with the Language of Seeing.

To start to learn the Language of Seeing, it's important to open your mind and turn your awareness level up. In other words, things you have seen and not paid attention to before may now become more important. Usually communication through this angel language appears quite subtly—although occasionally it comes in full force as Zechariah found out when he saw the vision in the Gospel of Luke in this chapter's opening verse. Most of the angel languages we study in this book will break down into two basic categories: the subtle and the overt. Overt messages are the easiest ones to notice. An example of this would be like seeing the actual form of an angel appearing above your bed and telling you what you need to do. Overt messages are the most obvious and undeniable, but they are rarer than subtle messages. Subtle messages are those we have to keep our awareness open to; we have to *look* for them rather than expecting them to jump out at us.

In my own case, I experienced a subtle but profound instance in the Language of Seeing shortly after the death of a loved one. My best friend Christine and I were making the 1,000-mile road trip to the cemetery where my loved one was buried, and we planned to do some sightseeing along the way to make the trip more fun.

One of our stops was at the Field of Dreams movie site in Dyersville, Iowa, where the iconic Kevin Costner movie of the same name was filmed. Costner plays a character who was estranged from his baseball-loving father before the father's death. For those of you that haven't seen it, one of the premises of the film is that there is life after death. In the movie, Costner's character is guided by a voice—the voice of an angel perhaps?—to build a baseball diamond in a cornfield on his farm in the middle of Iowa. The voice tells him, "If you build it, he will come." At the end of the movie Costner's character's father "appears" on the field, Costner joins him, and the broken relationship is healed.

For me, it was a fun side trip because that movie reminds me of my connections with the angels and it's in my home state. Shortly after our visit to the field and with the message of the movie fresh in our minds, Christine looked up and pointed to the sky. "Look, Kathy!" she said, "That cloud is changing colors!"

I looked up and saw a cloud that was rotating through tints of various colors, first pink, then green, and then blue, while all the other clouds around it remained white as snow.

This breathtaking display was truly amazing, and while we had no explanation for it, we knew it was a communication from the angels. But what could it mean? Christine and I stood together in the parking lot commenting back and forth on every new hue. We were mesmerized by the display and grateful we were both seeing exactly the same thing.

We continued on our journey, and a few days after we shared this experience, we finally made it to the cemetery. As I stood before my loved one's grave, an overwhelming sadness filled me. While I knew in my heart he was well and his spirit lived on, I also missed his bodily presence. As I pondered all of this, I began to cry. Christine stood by, supportive but helpless. There was nothing she could do to alleviate my grief. Even though I had been doing pretty well at not bottling up my emotions after my loved one's passing, somehow being at the cemetery opened a pit of grief within me that was far deeper than I had anticipated. Before I knew it, my tears had transformed into rattling sobs.

Christine gave me a few moments of privacy so that I could let these emotions out and busied herself walking around the cemetery. After several minutes she returned to my side. "Kathy, look," she said. "It's happening again." She pointed to the sky, and sure enough, there was a beautiful spot in the middle of the clouds that was beginning to change color, just as we had seen several hundred miles and several days earlier. At that moment I realized why we had seen the color-changing cloud after the visit to the Field of Dreams. This was a sign from the angels. I was being sent a message of comfort just as Costner's character had received in the movie: my loved one was fine. I looked around the cemetery, and it felt like I was seeing my own Field of Dreams. Through the Language of Seeing, I had been blessed once again by God's angelic handiwork. My tears dried and a sense of peace filled my heart.

I knew this message was a gift from my angels to support me through my loss. It reminded me how blessed I am to see signs from angels in the physical world. Because of my communication with the angels, I know that everyone who transitions to heaven is truly in a better place. Still, it's hard to be the person left here on the earth. I was so grateful the angels allowed me this beautiful sight that provided such comfort.

My experience seeing the clouds changing color is a subtle instance of the Language of Seeing. Not all examples are so subtle. For instance, I heard about a woman who went to the emergency room after developing sudden and acute pain in her abdomen. After running some tests, doctors delivered the bad news: they had located a large tumor. An emergency surgery followed soon after, but things did not go smoothly, leaving her in an intense amount of pain and with a cloudy prognosis.

Still in the hospital the night after the surgery, she awoke to a young woman in nurse's attire sitting at her bedside reading from the New Testament. As a Christian, she felt comforted by all this, but it also struck her as an unusual occurrence given that this was a secular hospital and it was the wee hours of the morning. She asked the woman, "Is everything okay?" To which the nurse replied, "Yes, I have come to make sure you are alright, and I can tell you that you will be well."

As the young nurse returned to reading aloud, the woman slowly drifted back to sleep. Upon waking the next morning, she asked the nurse on duty about her comforter, wanting to express her thanks for the unusual visit from the nurse with such compassionate bedside manner. The on-duty nurse gave her a puzzled look and explained that she had been on duty all night and was the only one who had entered her room. The woman, herself a believer in angels, suddenly knew without a doubt that the visitor had been an angel and the bearer of an important message. Just as the angel had said, the next batch of tests came back clean, and the doctors came to her with the good news that her situation had greatly improved during the night. Eventually she made a full recovery, with no lingering issues as a result of the tumor. Just as the angel had predicted, she was completely healed.

By learning some of the more common ways angels communicate with us visually, you can begin to learn and understand the Language of Seeing and utilize it in your everyday life.

Seeing the Signs

As Christine and I experienced on our road trip and in the cemetery, the Language of Seeing gives our angels an opportunity to come to us in a very profound way. To pick up on these messages, you must be on the lookout for them and maintain an open mind. For instance, you may not see anything "new" when you are seeking guidance. Instead, your eyes may be drawn to something you've seen many times before, only now that you understand the Language of Seeing, you will begin to view it and the things around you with a fresh perspective open to messages rather than just following a routine.

As in my own example, visual angel signs are often associated with clouds. Personally, I think this is because angels are from the heavens, and we are often told as children that heaven is "in the clouds." Not only do angels change the color of clouds, but they also communicate through their shapes as well. Many people have reported seeing the physical outline of an angel in the clouds, and others describe unusual shapes that have a personal symbolic meaning for them, usually something related to a situation they are dealing with in their lives at that moment.

The shape might answer a question you have about your life. For example, you may be asking, "Should I go forward with this plan of action?" and then see an octagon shape (better known as a STOP sign!). Or you may not spot a recognizable shape at all, but simply a cloud formation that for some unknown reason you find pleasing, comforting, and that evokes feelings of peace and satisfaction.

If you're worried you'll get a kink in your neck from staring at the sky waiting for a cloud message, never fear, because there are other dialects in the Language of Seeing. One is communication through numbers.

Biblical scholars have widely varying opinions on the meaning of numbers. Some believe that if you ascribe meaning to numbers, you are dabbling with divination, while others believe that certain numbers appear—and reappear!—in the Bible for a reason. (And don't forget, there's an entire book of the Bible named Numbers!)

The most common way angels use numbers to communicate is to put certain numbers in front of us repetitively. For instance, if I see a number three times or more in a short time span, I start to try and discern its meaning. If an answer doesn't come, I will specifically ask the angels to clarify their intended meaning via another sign.

As with all signs, it's also important to realize that the meanings associated with specific numbers can vary from person to person. The angels know this and act accordingly. For instance, if you see the number 3 or 33 consistently, and your child was born on March 3 (3/3), perhaps the message is a nudge to check on them. The number 3 could have an entirely different meaning for someone else. Through my years communicating with the angels, I have developed a list of numbers that are personally meaningful, so when I see repeating numbers, I have an idea of what the message might be. I highly recommend that you start your own list for easy reference.

In addition to numbers, you may have noticed times in your life when you start seeing the same items or images over and over. Maybe it was a type of car, a seemingly random image on a billboard or magazine, or any other image that keeps repeating. Just like with numbers, when the same objects or images keep appearing in your life, this can often be a message from the angels. In these situations, ask yourself, "Is there an area of my life that I need guidance on?" and "Is this repeating object I keep seeing a message for me?" The objects may be interpreted literally or symbolically. For example, a literal explanation of seeing a champagne glass over and over could be that there is an upcoming situation that involves alcohol. A symbolic meaning might be that you've done a job well and need to go celebrate. If you are unsure of the meaning, ask your angels for clarity and see what other message comes along.

The natural world is a favorite conduit for angels. If you find a feather, see a butterfly, or spot any type of animal that you don't normally see, this can often be a message from the angels. Feathers and butterflies are common ways angels use to show us they are always around, protecting us. When you see an animal that isn't common for your area, think about what quality or qualities are associated with that specific animal—the persistence of a turtle, for example—and see if there is anything going on in your life where those qualities are needed. For instance, if you see a fox, is there an area in your life where you need to be more skillful or cunning? If you see a goat, are you being stubborn about something? And if you see a serpent, is there a person or situation in your life that you need to take greater care around?

Growing up in Iowa, we watched expectantly for the first robin to return each spring. My mother got so excited each year when they arrived. To us it was a sign that spring was just around the corner—and after a dreary winter we really *needed* encouragement that spring was truly coming!

At the age of 97 my mom was put on hospice care. A few days after she was put in the program, I looked out my front window and saw a robin in the tree in my front yard! I knew the angels were telling me that she was going to have a peaceful transition to heaven. Her health declined rapidly, but I was fortunate to be with her during the last hours of her life. The morning after her passing, I looked out the front window, and was blessed to see another robin in the tree in my front yard! Those were the only two robins that I had seen! The message was clear to me: Mom was with the angels, and they were letting me know that all was well.

When you begin to spot the same numbers, objects, images, or uncommon sights in the natural world, I invite you to consider the possibility that these are not random coincidences but rather signs that have been divinely placed for you to receive. Once you have identified a sighting that is happening too often to be a coincidence or is too unusual to be random, the next step is to ask yourself what message is behind it. And when you aren't sure of the meaning in whatever you are seeing, it is absolutely okay to ask the angels for another sign. This is true for all the languages. If you don't understand or are unsure if what you are seeing, hearing, or feeling is a sign or you are unclear of its meaning, it's perfectly appropriate to request another one! Sometimes asking for further clarity is the only way we can understand to the fullest extent the message the angels are sending.

In addition to spotting subtler signs such as repeating or nonrandom occurrences, some people also can become aware of their angels from other visual cues, such as flashes of lights, shadows, or even silhouettes out of the corner of their eye. Others report getting sparkles of colored lights or white lights in their field of vision. These lights are usually found in one's peripheral vision, and generally your eyes are not focused on the area where the image occurs. Rather than providing you with a specific message, the purpose of these sightings is often just your angels letting you know that they are there for you. I find this very comforting, especially when I am having a rough day as I did at the cemetery.

Finally, don't underestimate the power of association, as where you are and who you are with can create an environment that is more conducive to visual signs. For example, my hairdresser loves angels just as much as I do, and she often asks them to be with her, which seems to me to be the reason why I see many visual reminders of angels (lights, sparkles in the corner of my eye, or silhouettes on the wall) when I'm in her chair.

As I mentioned earlier, angels will often appear in hospitals and other places where there is a greater need for their presence. Not surprisingly, angels are also seen in places where people are seeking a direct connection with them, such as a church, so remember this on Sundays!

Learning the Language of Seeing takes a willingness to view the physical world in a new and open-minded way. It's a departure from the scientific perspective of their being "random occurrences," and you open yourself to the idea that God's messengers want to make their presence known through signs available in your field of vision. As the New Testament clearly indicates, mysteries can be revealed to those who have "eyes... to see" (Mark 8:18). I invite you to speak the prayer at the end of this lesson to help you open your eyes to see God's heavenly angels.

Reflections

- Pray and ask God to help you develop your ability to communicate through the angelic Language of Seeing.

- Gaze through softened eyes. This helps to take your focus off of the physical world and may give the angels more opportunities to appear in your peripheral vision or out of the corner of your eye.

- When you see the same thing three times or more, start to view it as a potential sign and think on its meaning. If you're still confused, ask God for clarity around any message His angels are trying to give you.

Prayer

Lord God,

You created our eyes for seeing.

Help me to see both the visible and the invisible worlds through the Language of Seeing.

Help me to see Your plan for me in this world.

Pour Your blessings on me as I continue to learn the languages Your holy angels speak.

In the name of Your blessed son Jesus. Amen.

Chapter 4

The Language of Hearing

*Then I heard what sounded like a great
multitude, like the roar of rushing waters and
like loud peals of thunder, shouting:*

*"Hallelujah!
For our Lord God Almighty reigns.
Let us rejoice and be glad
and give him glory!"*
—Revelation 19:6–7

Throughout the Bible angels are found speaking to people from all walks of life. From Zechariah and Mary to the shepherds in the field, angels are recorded bringing us messages through the Language of Hearing. Along with the Language of Seeing, we encounter the Language of Hearing often throughout the Bible.

Like all the languages we will learn, the Language of Hearing can be divided into two parts: the subtle and the overt. To hear the subtler aspects of this language, you will begin by tuning in and listening with what I like to call your "angel ears."

Your angel ears can hear the angelic messages whether they come from the angels themselves or through other sources. For example, you may overhear a stranger speaking the words you need to hear, or a friend may call you at just the right time with just the right words, or a voice on the radio or the TV just "happens" to answer the question you were thinking about. This is similar to how you might see a billboard or cloud shape that might answer your question when you are tuned in to the Language of Seeing.

Another example of angel ears is when you hear the same song on the radio every time you get in the car, and the words or theme of the song have a message for you regarding a situation you are dealing with in your life. Hearing with your angel ears also refers to the "sound" of voices that you hear in your mind, like when you hear the same Bible verse over and over in your head. You may also hear sounds with your physical ears without being able to find the source, as happened to my friend Blanche.

Blanche received an auditory message from the angels a few months after she unexpectedly lost her husband. While trying to adapt the best she could to this tragedy, she found that she could not sleep well anymore. Night after night she tossed and turned, wondering if she would ever return to a normal sleep pattern again. One night as she was lying awake, she heard what sounded like a music box playing faintly in the distance. This was very strange because, as far as she knew, she didn't own a music box. She began walking through her home trying to uncover the source of the music. Finally, she determined that the music was loudest by her desk. She took each drawer out of the desk and emptied its contents one item at a time, but there was no music box to be found. Completely baffled, she began really listening to the music. It was then that she realized the song that was playing was "Silent Night." As she sat on the floor surrounded by the contents of her now empty desk, she began to sing along. When she got to the last line of the song, she received her message loud and clear: "Sleep in heavenly peace." The music stopped and she decided to return to her bed where she fell fast asleep, and from that night on her sleep was restored.

I heard another story about a woman who was dealing with a dear friend's illness. Toward the end of the friend's slow decline, the doctors predicted that her friend would not be alive for more than another six hours. Although her friend lived across the country, she knew she needed to be with her when she made her final transition. She caught the first flight she could and rented a car to embark on a long road trip to the small-town hospital where her friend was. Although the flight alone took three hours, she would need to drive another five, and the woman prayed that she would be able to see her friend just one more time. As she drove, Sarah McLaughlin's "Arms of the Angels" came on the radio. The woman felt reassured by the song and took it as a nod that she was doing the right thing—but then the strangest thing happened. She heard the song again. Then again. Then again. Within the span of forty-five minutes, the same song came across the radio four times, on different stations. She knew then that this was a sign from the angels that her friend was waiting for her to arrive before she herself went into the arms of her own angels. The song continued to play occasionally through the rest of her drive, and when the woman arrived, her friend was still alive and waiting for her so that they could be together when she passed on.

These messages came through music, but others have had experiences with angels speaking in ways that were anything but subtle. For instance, I once heard a story where a woman was driving with her three-year-old son in the backseat, back in the days before children's car seats. It was a warm day, and the air-conditioning was out, so the mother rolled down the windows to catch the breeze. Without warning, she heard a whisper that said, "Please roll up your son's window." Without questioning what she had heard, she rolled up the window and continued on the drive. As they went around a blind curve, they came face to face with another car coming at them head-on. She jerked on the steering wheel to swerve out of the way and lost control of the car as they were sent into a spin and flipped several times. The car ended up on its side. Miraculously, although he was pressed up against the window, her son was unhurt. However, if that window had still been rolled down, he likely would have fallen through it or been thrown from the car in the collision.

This next story you have likely already heard, as it was well publicized on national news. Four police officers heard a woman's cries for help coming from inside a crashed car. All four of the officers heard the same thing: the desperate pleas for help from inside the overturned vehicle. When they cut the car open to rescue the victims of the accident, they discovered that only a small child, an eighteen-month-old girl, had survived. The driver and only other person in the car, the girl's mother, had died on impact over fourteen hours before the police arrived! And yet they all *still* heard the same voice of a grown woman calling from the wreck. This experience completely baffled the officers, but they heard what they heard! In my view it's clear that the spirit of the woman was working in tandem with the Lord's angels to reach the officers in order to save her infant daughter.

As a final example, I was honored to briefly know a beautiful, gracious woman who had many health problems. As her health deteriorated, she remained a pillar of light and love. I visited her shortly after she had gotten the news that her cancer was incurable. We knew that her days were numbered, yet the peace that she exuded was incredible, because, as she told me, she had invited the angels to be with her in this time of transition. She smiled and said, "I can hear the angels. They're gathering in the hall to take me home. They'll be here when it's time for me to go." She was hearing the angels' wings brushing against the walls of her home. She was never afraid of what she was hearing because she knew that the Lord and the angels were connecting with her in a way that would make her passing as peaceful as possible.

Hearing the Message

As these stories demonstrate, the messages from angels in the Language of Hearing can arrive subtly or overtly. In my own case, I initially thought that the voice I would hear when the angels spoke directly to me would be a big, booming, male voice, but that has not been in my experience nor the experience for the many others who have shared their stories with me. Verbal messages from the angels often sound like our own voice or the voice of someone we are close to. The sound itself may come from inside of us (an unspoken message or one that occurs only in your mind and does not come through your physical ears) or outside of us (a spoken message coming through your physical ears).

The message you hear may come to you loudly or softly, either with subtlety or in a blatant way, but most importantly the voice of the angels will always be positive and loving. I want to be absolutely clear on this point: angels only say kind and helpful things, it is never their intention to frighten their listeners, and they will only ever deliver messages that are supportive and advantageous for you. Even if they are giving you a warning or correcting you, the angels' message will not be given to you in a scary way.

Quite often when angels speak directly to a person, they will first assure their listener that there is no need to be afraid. It's easy to imagine how it might be frightening to suddenly hear a booming angelic voice, especially when you don't know where it's coming from, and I have spoken to several people who mentioned how startled they were when an angelic voice first began to speak to them! Imagine how surprised Zechariah must have been on hearing the angel Gabriel speaking to him in the Book of Luke.

But the angel said to him: "Do not be afraid, Zechariah; your prayer has been heard. Your wife Elizabeth will bear you a son, and you are to call him John." (Luke 1:13)

First and foremost, Gabriel asks Zechariah to not be afraid before he delivers his message. This speaks to the fact that the angels have no intention of terrifying us, but also recognize the fact that their presence is powerful and can be uncomfortable or startling when it comes out of the blue.

Subtle messages in the Language of Hearing are the messages that come to us from sources other than angels, such as through a friend, a TV announcement, or a radio advertisement. Another way that angels bring us subtle auditory messages is through a ringing in one ear. This is not tinnitus (a medical condition involving a constant ringing in the ears), although it is often mistaken for it, and it happens in only one ear at a time for a relatively short amount of time. For me, this means that the angels are bringing me information I will need in the future, so it serves as a sign that a message is being sent. When I need the information, it is always there, so I trust the angel's process in giving me their message in this way.

As happened with my friend Blanche who lost her husband, I have found that we're often more receptive to hearing the voice of God and the angels when we are lying down resting or just starting to wake up. When our brains are resting, God and the angels can come through more easily because they don't have to find a way to bypass our thinking minds. When you are asking for angelic guidance, try this idea: when you say your prayers at night, ask God the question you are seeking an answer to and invite Him to send the angels to you to help you hear His message. Then, go to sleep!

The angels may bring you guidance in your dreams, as we'll cover in chapter 7, but the purpose of this bedtime invitation is aimed at a message the following morning. Take your time waking up. I advise waking as gradually and naturally as possible—or at least using an alarm clock with a soothing rather than a panicked sound to help you move slowly into wakefulness. This is when the angels can bring messages to you through the Language of Hearing, when all else is quiet in your home and in your mind and they can bypass your constantly churning brain. As you wake, be aware of any sounds, songs, music, or voices that may come to you in these moments of reflection. Remember that the angels' signs may be as blatant as a voice in your ear or as subtle as the music on your radio alarm clock. Be open to receiving the messages they bring.

In Mark 8:18 Jesus talks about those who have "ears but fail to hear," which seems to be the root of the problem when it comes to receiving angelic messages in the Language of Hearing. I think for many of us the main difficulty we have in connecting with our angels is that we don't invite them in and allow for them to guide us in our lives. Doing so is paramount to opening our spiritual ears in order to receive messages from Jesus and His angels.

The Language of Hearing is available to all of us, if only we will ask the angels to speak to us and nurture our relationship with them with daily dialogues (even if they seem one-sided at first). Messages delivered through the Language of Hearing may come overtly through spoken or unspoken means or subtly through things we may overhear in our everyday life, but the key to receiving angelic messages in this and all the other angel languages is to ask and allow the angels to send their messages through you. With an invitation to bring you guidance, your angels will always be ready and willing to bring you whatever messages will serve your best interest. The prayer at the end of this chapter will help you do exactly that.

Reflections

- Ask God to help you open your angel ears.

- Remember that you may hear the voice inside your head. It may not be audible to others.

- On days that you can, wake up slowly. It's more difficult for God's angels to bring us messages when we're rushing!

- Develop your personal connection with the angels and invite them to bring you messages through the Language of Hearing—then make the time for them to do so by sitting in stillness and quiet with your request for guidance.

Prayer

Lord,

*Thank You for the verbal messages
that Your loving angels bring me.*

*Open my ears. Let me hear their voices.
Open my heart to know You even
better through the messages I receive
from Your beautiful, loving angels.*

In Jesus' name. Amen.

Chapter 5

The Language of Feeling

*Suddenly an angel of the Lord appeared and
a light shone in the cell. He struck Peter on
the side and woke him up . . .*

—Acts 12:7

When I begin describing the different languages angels use to communicate with us, some people discover that they're already receiving messages, most often through the Language of Feeling. Because it's sometimes already occurring and only needs to be recognized, the Language of Feeling is one of the most popular methods for people to initially find their angel connection. It certainly was for me!

The Language of Feeling can be broken down into two major components: physical feelings (such as a tap on the shoulder) and emotional feelings (such as anxiety or delight). The physical language is when angels communicate with us through our tactile senses (rather than by sight or by hearing). This can take any form, such as getting goose bumps at a strange time, the sensation of a hand brushing your hair, or of someone settling next to you on the couch. The physical aspect of this language can be subtle or overt. An example of overt physical components might be something as blatant as a tap on the shoulder or as abstruse as a tickle in your hair. I've heard stories of people who have experienced very obvious physical communication from the angels. One young man who was crossing the street around a blind corner didn't see the car coming his way before it was already on him, horn honking. Suddenly he felt a force on his chest that pushed him back up onto the curb. There was no one in front of him, but this angelic push undoubtedly saved his life.

While the physical Language of Feeling is the easiest to notice and explain, I want to be clear that the Language of Feeling can also include emotions, and these are almost always in the realm of subtle signs. For instance, when thinking about your next step in life, do you feel peace or anxiety? Do you feel excited or nervous? Frustrated or delighted? We are often taught to consider what we "think" over what we "feel." Our society puts a higher value on what thoughts we have rather than what feelings come to us. However, if you've ever had a "gut feeling" without rational thought behind it, you already know just how powerful the Language of Feeling can be. To me, a sense of happiness or wholeness shows when I'm on the right track, whereas the "wrong track" will feel disappointing or hollow. In both cases, our angels use our emotions to guide us.

For example, one woman I know had a very telling experience with her gut feelings that I believe was a sign from the angels. She was working in a very demanding and fast-paced job which she loved. As time went on, certain changes were made within the company, and she found that she was loving her job less and less. It got to the point where she would wake up each morning with a feeling of dread and despair at the thought of going to work. When she considered quitting her job though, she felt a sense of peace and ease. Although her logical mind could point to a thousand reasons why she shouldn't quit—most of them around maintaining her financial well-being—she kept having this nagging impression that she needed to take a leap of faith.

Her friends and family all begged her to keep working even though the job was grinding her down, if only until she found something else, but she knew in her heart that she needed to make a change and that continuing on at her job would only bring more negativity into her life. After praying over the decision for several weeks, she found that she *felt* infinitely better when she pictured her life without this job, and she felt guided to give her two weeks' notice. She saw the effects of quitting immediately—suddenly she was smiling again, she was enjoying her life, and her creative flow returned. It was through this creative flow that she was able to change careers entirely, to a new line which brought her more passion—and eventually even greater financial success—than her old job ever did. Her analytical mind had told her that to quit her job could only bring ruin, but the angels spoke to her through the language of feeling, *through* her feelings, and guided her to her best path and out of a negative situation.

God created feelings—physical sensations as well as emotions—and He can use His angels to speak to us through them. Sometimes the Language of Feeling will speak to us from both the physical and the emotional sides at the same time. I read a story once about a woman who was pregnant with twins. Only two weeks before her scheduled C-section, her water broke and she became afraid because she could no longer feel the babies moving or kicking in her belly. She was rushed to the hospital where the babies were delivered immediately via emergency C-section, but one of the babies and the mom were both touch and go. As I mentioned previously, angels many times will reach out to us in places where they are needed the most—such as in hospitals—and that is exactly what happened to this mom. While she was slipping in and out of consciousness following her surgery, she felt comforted by a presence beside her, despite the fact that none of her family had made it to the hospital. This was a subtle feeling of solace, but she was also physically comforted, as occasionally she awoke feeling someone straightening her blankets, tucking her in, or stroking her hand. As she and both babies grew stronger, these instances lessened. Finally, as their hospital stay was coming to a close, she decided she needed to repay the special nurse who had attended to her and her babies and provided so much comfort during their stay. She asked the head nurse of her ward to help her identify what nurse had been sitting with her during those long nights, but was baffled when she was told that no one had stayed with her overnight. She stared blankly at the head nurse in confusion—but the head nurse, who had seen a few angelic miracles herself, only smiled a knowing smile and gave the most simple and profound explanation: "No one is truly alone. Our angels are always with us when we need them."

Feeling the Angels around You

We can get a variety of messages from our angels through the Language of Feeling. They may tell us to move forward with our plans or to pull back from them. Sometimes we get a "thumbs up" and sometimes a "thumbs down." By paying close attention to how you feel and becoming more aware of the presence of angels around you, you will be able to discern more of God's messages through the angels' Language of Feeling. It takes time to grow accustomed to this, so be patient with yourself as you're learning how to connect with your angels. After all these years, even I'm still finding out more about communicating with my angels in this language!

For instance, have you ever gotten goose bumps when you're not cold? That was how my first angel experience started. Some people I know call goose bumps "truth bumps" or "God bumps." When this happens to me, I know it is a huge "yes" from the angels that whatever I'm thinking about at that exact moment is the right path for me. I can be outside sweating in the hot Texas summer sun, but if the angels start communicating with me, I get goose bumps.

Apparently my goose bumps are impressive because they're so obvious. One time I was in the middle of talking to a friend about the messages I received from angels, and as I talked to her, the goose bumps started coming. Her eyes got huge when she spotted them up and down my arms and realized what was happening.

The biggest problem we have in communicating through the Language of Feeling is when we discount what we are sensing—either physically or emotionally. For instance, I've known people who will say, "Oh, I just felt someone brush my hair! It was probably just the wind." It may very well have been the wind—but if you've asked for angelic guidance, this sensation may not be just a coincidence. Being aware of the physical sensations we experience as well as our emotions is the key to the Language of Feeling. A message from your angels will feel loving, expansive, and kind. It's the same sensation you get with a warm hug. You will feel safe. Your emotions and senses will be consistent. If you have vacillating emotions about what to do, this is not your angels speaking but likely your mind intruding and trying to offer its own advice. If you find yourself waffling on what to do and are not sure if you're interpreting the angels' signals correctly, ask them to be more clear. They are always happy to help you get the message that you need, even if that means bringing it to you in a different form.

The way angels touch us physically can vary. Sometimes it may feel like an angel is hugging you, while at other times it may be a touch on the shoulder as in 1 Kings 19:5: "All at once an angel touched him. . . ." I experience an emotional warmth in my heart or my stomach when the angels are using the Language of Feeling to deliver a message that I am on the right track. Conversely, when I get a cold or disconnected feeling,

I know that I need to be aware and alert and perhaps rethink any choice I have in front of me.

The angels will employ physical and emotional feelings together, so pay attention to the emotions that arise during the moments when you feel their physical presence, as this is how they guide you toward the correct message. For instance, let's say you feel the angels tickle your hair. When this happens to a close friend of mine, she simultaneously feels comforted and reassured, which is a signal that she's on the right track and is receiving God's love and guidance.

There are so many different ways the angels can reach out to you using the Language of Feeling. That's why I ask you to be patient with yourself as you learn more about this. Remember, your angels will be patient with you too! They're so glad that you're working on connecting with them.

Sometimes the angels speak to me through what I call "angel grins." It's kind of hard to explain, but it is what happens when I start smiling but I'm not the one who made my mouth muscles move. It's a funny feeling when the corners of your mouth start to turn up and you're not willing it yourself. My angel grins are bigger than my normal smile. When they happen, I feel light and happy. I can tell the angels are rejoicing around me. By this same token, when angels also speak to me by making the muscles of my body feel tight or closed, that's a sign to reexamine any path or action I am currently taking.

Recently my angels started working with me in a new way. They move my toes up in the air, and just like the angel grins, I'm not the one causing it. I have learned there are three different meanings when this happens:

1. Anticipation—I'm being told of a happy upcoming experience.

2. An alert or a warning—I am around a person I need to be wary of.

3. They want me to help someone.

How I determine which message I'm getting is by how I feel emotionally when it happens. Anticipation feels happy, while warnings make me anxious.

It is helpful to look to the Language of Feeling when you need to make a choice but you truly can't decide what to do. This language is so great for decisions because it asks you to bypass your "thinking" mind and go deep into the sensations and emotions that God and the angels are providing for you.

To use the Language of Feeling to make decisions, find a few minutes of private time and a quiet space. Settle in comfortably, and give yourself a few moments to tune in. When you're ready, pray on the subject that you're concerned about, and remember to ask for God's guidance. As we talked about before, the angels can't help us unless we ask for their help, so don't be shy to say, "Lord, I need your help. Please allow Your angels to show me Your guidance." With your eyes closed, visualize each of the choices that are in front of you. Take your time and notice how your body feels when you dive deep into each choice. Usually one choice will feel better than the other (either physically somewhere in your body or emotionally). This is your angels speaking to you through the Language of Feeling by giving you a warm, happy, comfortable, or satisfied response to one of the choices. If one choice stands out as feeling good to you, then that is the option you are being guided to select. If no choice stands out or if they all cause you the same level of satisfaction or dissatisfaction, try asking God and the angels the same question from a broader perspective. Instead of asking "which of these options is best?" try "what is best for me in this moment?" It may very well be that there is another option you haven't seen yet, and the angels are only waiting for you to ask so that they can show you a different path.

Remember that the feelings that come from your angels will always be consistent, whether they are physical sensations or emotional responses or both. The answer will be clear and true for you across both spectrums of the Language of Feeling. Now that we have a grasp of the Language of Feeling, let's move into discussing a language that functions very similarly with a few key differences: the Language of Knowing.

Reflections

- Pray and ask God to help you develop the Language of Feeling.

- Be aware of the natural feelings that arise within you throughout the day. Do not push them down. Be aware and ask God what His angels may be trying to tell you.

- Consciously relax throughout the day. I find that people lose touch with their feelings due to the hectic pace of their day. Pause. Relax. Notice your feelings.

Prayer

Lord of the Universe!

*Thank You for Your angels who speak to
me through the Language of Feeling.*

*Help me to learn all of the ways they speak to
me. I want to receive Your messages from them.*

I want to do Your will.

In Jesus' name. Amen.

Chapter 6

The Language of Knowing

*Then you will know the truth, and the
truth will set you free.*

—John 8:32

Despite certain similarities to the Language of Feeling, the Language of Knowing is often the hardest for people to understand. Somehow when people feel, see, or hear the angels, the messages and modes of communication seem more tangible. People who experience the Language of Knowing often discount it because it isn't "as good" or as "spectacular" as seeing, hearing, or feeling angelic presences. They assume that if they know things, everyone else does too. This is not the case. The Language of Knowing is a very powerful gift and needs to be acknowledged as such.

When I talk to people about the Language of Knowing, it usually turns out to be a fairly short conversation. *A person with the gift of knowing just knows things. They don't have a reason why or how they know things, they just know.* That pretty much sums up this entire chapter! However, I'll try to flesh things out a little further, as sometimes the simplest concepts can be the most difficult to integrate.

The Language of Knowing is when you experience a deep inner drive to do something and you are compelled to complete it. For example, with the Language of Knowing you might have an idea for a project that you can't let go of. Your idea might be a business you want to start, a recurring thought to call a friend you haven't spoken to in a while, or the idea that you need to visit a loved one *right now*. And like all the languages, the Language of Knowing can be either subtle or overt.

I experienced a subtle (and humorous) occurrence of my own a few years ago. I was approaching a milestone birthday and felt the need to celebrate by doing something I'd never done before. Someone suggested skydiving, but I'm not a daredevil, so that was out of the question. Another suggested a tattoo, but I didn't want something permanently emblazoned on my body. Neither of these ideas, nor many of the others I received, resonated with me. Then someone suggested that I buy a fitted toe ring—don't laugh!—to commemorate the occasion. The moment I heard this idea I *knew* it was what I needed to do. It was like a lightbulb going off in my head! *This* was what I had to do!

On my birthday my daughter and I went to get our toe rings. The minute the ring was placed on my toe I had another insight. The idea came to me like a lightning strike with such force and vehemence that it was impossible to ignore: I needed to start a toe ring business. This was beyond odd for me, since this was my first experience with toe rings, but I knew—I mean I really *KNEW*—that I needed to do it! I could not get the idea out of my head.

Well, I did exactly that. On nothing more than a *knowing* that the toe ring business was for me, I started my own company. To this day, I love the company I created, and it's still a profitable source of income. I felt that deep inner knowing and followed it, which has continued to bless me with a fun source of revenue.

Some of my friends have experienced messages as simple as knowing it's going to rain (and bringing an umbrella to outings!) despite the forecast calling for sunshine. These instances can be amusing—even silly for the rest of us who get caught in the rain—but other times knowings take on a more serious quality. Consider the story of my friend Shari who knew she was called to go to law school. She applied to several schools, and received a "wait-list" letter from one of them. She had prayed and *knew* this was the school she was meant to go to, and even when she was going to start. She packed a week's worth of clothing in her car, and made the four-hour drive to the school, far from her hometown. Without an appointment, she walked into the admissions office and asked to meet the Dean of Admissions. She told him that she was meant to start law school, and that her life purpose was to help children with disabilities and their families be treated fairly in court. She asked him to look at her application and admit her to the school. Though he sent her back to the lobby, after waiting for quite a long time she got up and marched back into his office and sat down, determined. With her sitting right in front of him, he had no choice but to review her application in front of her. Finally, he looked up at her and said, "Welcome to law school." She is now a practicing attorney doing her best to right the wrongs that happen in this world. Her *absolute knowing* led to her making a gutsy move that helped not only herself, but the world.

Other subtle examples of the Language of Knowing include such instances as when you are in a store and just *know* you need to buy a certain item, though it makes no logical sense to you. You buy it, and later in the day you run into someone who needs it but could not have afforded it themselves. Or you might have a deep compulsion to say something specific to a person you are speaking to, and in the course of the conversation you find out you used the exact words they needed to hear.

Sometimes the Language of Knowing comes with a deep sense of urgency around it, in a way which is more overt. This happened to my friend Cheryl. She wrote about the experience and has been gracious enough to allow me to share it in her own words:

> *My father was in a specialty rehab hospital. Luckily my brother, Cameron, worked close to the hospital and visited him at lunch daily. I visited after work. It worked well for us, and we got to see our father every day.*
>
> *Around 11:00 a.m. one morning I had a sudden urge to go check on my father. I did not hear a voice, feel a sensation, or have anything physically significant happen. I just knew I needed to leave at that moment and I did. When I arrived at my father's room, a therapist was standing over my father with tears rolling down her cheeks. I asked what was wrong. She told me my father had*

forgotten how to drink from a straw and was blowing instead of sucking. Then she said, "Something is terribly wrong today." She told me she had called for the nurse, but she hadn't come. I immediately went down the hall and found the RN. She came in the room, realized my father needed immediate attention, and called a code blue. Medical personnel rushed in and started working on my father. About that time Cameron came in and asked if I had been called to the hospital. I told him I had not, but simply had the feeling I needed to get there. I was able to call my other brother, Lyndon, and get my mother there in time to see him before they rushed him to the emergency room at the main hospital. My father went to heaven to rejoice with the angels at 3:00 p.m. I'm so glad I got there in time to be with my father and hear him comfort us saying "it's okay, everything is okay."

The Language of Knowing can generate some very important messages, as in Cheryl's case. She didn't have any physical or logical evidence that she needed to go to see her father before their usual visitation time, but by acting on the knowing she received from the angels, she was able to be with her father before his passing.

Sometimes the Language of Knowing can even save lives. For instance, I have heard stories of medical professionals and specifically midwives who work in remote areas of the world where standard hospital equipment and practices are not available. In these situations, many midwives have described a feeling of "knowing" of what to do when complications arise. In part it is their medical training that leads them to make decisions that are best and appropriate for their patients, but specifically in situations that they are unfamiliar with or have not encountered previously, many have described a solution occurring to them out of the blue as an aha moment, which led to a correct diagnosis or helped them to make the proper medical decisions even when all the variables of the situation were clouded.

Subtly guiding a doctor's hand isn't the only way the Language of Knowing can save lives though. There was a woman who lived in the Deep South, in the town she had grown up in her whole life. Her father lived on the other side of town, and although her mother had passed away some time before, her ninety-year-old father continued to live on his own. One day as she was driving home from work, she suddenly *knew* that she had to see him. Trying to fight it since his house was in the opposite direction of her commute, she phoned him three times, but he never answered. After leaving the third voice mail and unable to shake the compelling thought that she needed to go physically see him, she sighed and turned the car around. She expected to find him asleep in his armchair with his hearing aids out when she arrived, but she would at least be able to put this persistent nagging suspicion to bed. When she arrived, he didn't answer the door, so she went through the unlocked backyard, only to find her father on the ground where he had fallen some hours before while gardening. He was dehydrated from the summer sun and in pain, but the woman was able to call an ambulance and he got the help he needed. If she had continued to ignore the knowing that she received from the angels, he might very well have been more seriously hurt or could have died if no one had come to his home to discover his fall. As you can see, the Language of Knowing is a *very* powerful language indeed!

What Do You Know?

The Language of Knowing speaks deep in your heart. In Joshua 23:14, Joshua is giving his farewell when he says, *". . . You know with all your heart and soul that not one of all the good promises the LORD your God gave you has failed. Every promise has been fulfilled; not one has failed."* While this Bible verse is not specifically about the Language of Knowing, it points to the depth of this angel language. Joshua knows with all his heart and soul, not with his thinking mind or his rational logic, but a deep understanding that comes from his connection with God. That's the Language of Knowing!

The best way to create space for the Language of Knowing is to suspend your disbelief—and any other beliefs! For instance, if you are struck by a sudden aha moment where you feel clarity around something that was originally murky, you should certainly be discerning on whether or not this is a message from the angels or a trick of the mind, but also be careful not to close yourself up to the possibility that this knowing is more than just a spark in your brain. Messages that come from the Language of Knowing will be repetitive, consistent signs that make sense and will usually be accompanied by a sense of excitement. If you have a sudden knowing that you should quit your job, but you feel terrified by the prospect, this isn't your angels talking. Your knowings from the angels will be loving, consistent, and make sense.

I have found that the knowings I receive from the angels move in my mind differently than my own thoughts. For example, if it is one of my own thoughts, it generally slides off my mind very easily, so I have to write things down to be sure I don't forget. However, when it comes to angelic knowings, they stick in the forefront of my mind and are with me until I act on them.

There's no way to *force* knowings to come to you; it isn't the same as a conscious thought where you can muddle over something for days on end until a solution presents itself. The Language of Knowing is usually spontaneous and immediate—but there are a few ways that you can create more space to connect with the knowings that may come to you.

One way to create space for the angels to communicate via the Language of Knowing is to meditate or sit in silent prayer. Find a place where you can have some comfortable privacy—even if that means going into the bathroom and locking the door. Sit or lie down so that your physical body is comfortable—and therefore not distracting you—and take several deep breaths. As you focus on your breathing, invite the angels to be with you and to bring you guidance on whatever problem is on your mind. Try not to jump on a hamster wheel of rehashing your problem over and over, simply bring it to God in your prayer and then remain still and silent. The intention of this exercise isn't to necessarily receive answers—though they absolutely might come as soon as you are still!—but to put some distance between you and the busyness of your day and the stress of your current situation. When you give the situation up to God's hands, God will bring you the guidance and wisdom you need. I have found that this works particularly well for the Language of Knowing because when I can silence my own mind, which can spiral into an out-of-control pattern of worry and doubt, it becomes easier for me to receive God in my mind and for the knowings that He sends me through the angels to become clear. I think of it like a crowded room: God's guidance is being whispered to me through the chatter of my own thoughts, but it isn't until I can silence all of the background noise my thoughts are creating that I can know what God has intended for me.

The Language of Knowing is one of the hardest to intentionally practice, but it is best to keep your mind open to allow other knowings to come to you. This is a *very* powerful angel language, although it is over discounted because it's less "flashy" and sometimes harder to identify. Trust what you know, and trust that you know what you know for a reason. Then, take action. Have faith that God's holy angels are bringing you the messages you need to receive through the Language of Knowing!

Reflections

- Go into prayer and ask God to help you learn the angel Language of Knowing.

- Allow for the possibility that angels may already be giving you messages through the Language of Knowing. Ask yourself: "Do I often know things that others don't know? Are the angels already using this language with me?"

- When you feel an urgency to say or do something, trust that you need to do it. Take action.

Prayer

Lord,

*I want to know You more! I want to
receive Your messages through
the Language of Knowing.*

*Help me to trust the messages
I receive from Your angels.*

Help me take action on them.

*Help me bless the world through
the ideas and inspiration
Your angels bring me.*

*In the precious name of Your son Jesus.
Amen.*

Chapter 7

The Language of Dreams and Visions

"We both had dreams," they answered,
"but there is no one to interpret them."
Then Joseph said to them, "Do not
interpretations belong to God?
Tell me your dreams."
—Genesis 40:8

The angel of God said to me in the dream,
"Jacob." I answered, "Here I am."
—Genesis 31:11

I'm often asked what the difference is between dreams and visions. I have dreams when I'm asleep and visions when I'm awake (though you can have visions with your eyes open or closed—that part doesn't matter). Visions can sometimes be confused with messages that really fall under the Language of Seeing, and we will discuss the differences in a moment, but in general, don't worry about categorizing them correctly, just be glad the messages are coming through!

Most dreams and visions are symbolic, not literal. We see an example of this in Zechariah 1:18–19:

Then I looked up, and there before me were four horns. I asked the angel who was speaking to me, "What are these?" He answered me, "These are the horns that scattered Judah, Israel and Jerusalem."

The four horns were symbolic of Jerusalem being scattered. They were not meant to be taken literally. This is important to keep in mind as you start investigating your dreams and visions. Many of our dreams don't make much sense literally, but when we view them as symbols for the other things that are going on in our lives, suddenly the pieces begin to fall into place.

Here's one of my angelic dreams that I remember the most vividly and the symbolic interpretation that I discerned from it. I dreamt I was walking by a church, and I could hear a lamb bleating inside. I knew the lamb was hungry and had been without food for several days, so I went inside to feed it. When I opened the door, I saw people inside the church, and I couldn't understand why they hadn't fed the lamb. When I woke up, I spent all day praying to discern the dream correctly. Finally that night I suddenly realized that I was the one who needed to "feed the lambs!" That was it! I was to feed the Lord's lambs, just as Jesus asked of Peter in John 21:17:

The third time he said to him, "Simon son of John, do you love me?" Peter was hurt because Jesus asked him the third time, "Do you love me?" He said, "Lord, you know all things; you know that I love you." Jesus said, "Feed my sheep."

Then, of course—God works this way a lot—my pastor preached on that text the very next day! God was calling me to feed His lambs by teaching them about angels. The dream I had was consistent with the other signs I was receiving through other angel languages, so I knew it was a signal from them. Though this is one of the most prominent dreams I've had, the angels also have spoken to me in visions when I am awake as well, in a very profound and *definitive way.*

Visions occur when we are awake and can best be characterized as something appearing suddenly in our mind's eye. This is how I distinguish visions from physical manifestations that are really a communication in the first language we learned, the Language of Seeing. When the angels are communicating with me using the Language of Seeing, I am actually seeing something in the physical world. When something suddenly appears in my mind but I know it's not "out in the world," then I call it a vision.

For example, my friend Jen and I decided to take a trip to a family vacation home in West Texas one December, what we called a year-end spiritual retreat. She is also in touch with the angels, and together we enjoyed their healing presence in our quiet getaway.

Then two nights before we were to leave, snow started to fall. Remember we were in West Texas, and while snowfall isn't unheard of there, it certainly isn't the norm, especially as early as December. The next morning—the day before we were going to head home—we checked the weather and the road conditions. Travel was not advised. The interstate leading home had iced over in several spots. We hoped it would clear up within the next twenty-four hours and held to our plans to leave the next morning.

In the morning, we checked the road conditions again. Travel was still not advised. On top of that, there was a winter storm approaching with even more ice. The weather was forecast to stay below freezing for several more days. We either had to disregard the travel advisory or be stranded in the house for up to a week!

Since I was the one driving, Jen left the decision up to me. We sat down and prayed for guidance. As we finished the prayer and I opened my eyes, the words "Go now!" materialized in my mind, just as clear as a bright sunny day. I don't like driving on ice, but I couldn't ignore the message: it was a vision from the angels! I told Jen we needed to leave immediately! We couldn't get into the car fast enough, and soon we were on the road.

We prayed the entire way, and the angels guided us and kept us safe. There were numerous cars in ditches all along the road, but our timing turned out to be perfect. We were able to drive through the previously closed patch of highway right after the road workers had cleared it of ice and just before any more ice could build up. If we had left an hour earlier, the road would not have been cleared. If we had left any later, we would have been caught in the upcoming storm. It was a very tough and tiring drive, but we made it home safely.

The next day we learned that friends of the family who owned the home had been stranded in the area in the incoming storm, and they used the house as their shelter while they waited it out. Had we not left when we did, we would have been living in the house with five people we didn't know very well for several days. By inviting the angels to offer their guidance, we received their message through a vision that I could not ignore, telling us exactly when we needed to leave in order to make it home safely.

I've had many different visions and dreams over the years, and I haven't always gotten the meaning right on the first shot. One time I was so slow to implement the angel's message that I received similar visions three times before I finally took the correct action.

The first vision was three cords coming out of an electrical outlet. To me the number three means the Trinity—Father, Son, and Holy Spirit—and an electrical outlet meant that I needed to recharge. I discerned that God was telling me that I needed to take a break. Being *occasionally* stubborn, I didn't.

The next day I had a vision of a "do not disturb" sign on a door. I interpreted this vision to mean that I needed to rest. I did not rest.

The third day I had a vision of a hole in my car's engine that went through the floorboards into the driver's side of the car right where I sit. I discerned that my "engine" was broken, and I needed to rest! At that point I knew it was really important for me to slow down and take a break. Since the angels weren't letting me ignore this message no matter how stubbornly I tried, I set aside time for a much-needed vacation and felt much better when I got back into the swing of things.

These visions were consistent. They came three days in a row. Each time the message was the same even though the imagery was different. Our angels *are* very consistent. They keep repeating themselves until we listen to them. Don't let your hardheadedness get in the way! Life is much easier when we pay attention and follow our angels' messages immediately.

Some people also experience dreams that bring them messages of comfort, which is something the angels are always trying to do for us. A woman had this experience after a close friend died abruptly in a drunk driving accident. A few months into her grieving, the woman was beginning to recover but something still held her back from fully moving on. One night after she went to bed, she had a dream. Her friends were all sitting in her living room, where they met every week in real life. The friend who had passed, Larry, was absent, but this absence wasn't unusual to her in life or in dreams anymore. Then there was a knock at the door. She excused herself and answered it, only to find Larry standing there, grinning. She was happy to see him and quickly invited him in—she never felt shocked or frightened by his sudden appearance, just glad to see him. She gave him a hug and asked what had taken him so long. Larry, with his prankster's smile, just beamed and told her that everything was fine. When she woke up, she felt an immediate sense of peace, as though she had just received a big bear hug from her friend, and used this dream message that the angels had sent her about her friend as the final push to move forward in her life and let go of the grief she was still holding on to.

Because I know that dreams are one of the more controversial aspects of angel communication—critics claim they are "just dreams"—I want to take a moment and point out two stories in the Bible that demonstrate to us how important they actually are.

One person who is often associated with dreams in the Bible is Joseph from the Old Testament. Joseph was visited by dreams from God that helped him to advise his family, which led his brothers to sell him into slavery out of jealousy. While he was imprisoned, Joseph began to translate the dreams his fellow prisoners had and, as his predictions came true, gained enough renown as a dream interpreter that he was summoned to interpret Pharaoh's dreams:

Pharaoh said to Joseph, "I had a dream, and no one can interpret it. But I have heard it said of you that when you hear a dream you can interpret it." "I cannot do it," Joseph replied to Pharaoh, "but God will give Pharaoh the answer he desires." (Genesis 41:15–16)

Based on Joseph's dream interpretation which predicted seven years of abundance followed by seven years of famine, Pharaoh made Joseph his vizier, in charge of keeping the people of Egypt from starvation even in the midst of the seven years of famine.

Another Joseph also followed the guidance God brought to him in dreams. Joseph of the New Testament, husband to Mary, had dreams that changed the history of the world. Through his dreams he chose to marry Mary, kept Jesus safe by escaping to Egypt, brought Jesus and Mary back to Israel when Herod was dead, and moved the family to Nazareth, fulfilling the Old Testament prophecy. Thank heavens he listened to and followed the messages he got in his dreams!

This is how the birth of Jesus the Messiah came about: His mother Mary was pledged to be married to Joseph, but before they came together, she

was found to be pregnant through the Holy Spirit.
Because Joseph her husband was faithful to the
law, and yet did not want to expose her to public
disgrace, he had in mind to divorce her quietly. But
after he had considered this, an angel of the Lord
appeared to him in a dream and said, "Joseph son
of David, do not be afraid to take Mary home as
your wife, because what is conceived in her is from
the Holy Spirit. She will give birth to a son, and
you are to give him the name Jesus because he
will save his people from their sins." All this took
place to fulfill what the Lord had said through the
prophet: "The virgin will conceive and give birth
to a son, and they will call him Immanuel (which
means 'God with us')." (Matthew 1:18–23)

Dream a Little Dream

As these biblical stories indicate, dreams, just like angels, have an important place in Christian history. But why do God and the angels come to us in dreams anyway? With all the angel languages, we have to be open to receiving God's messages, and this is often easiest when our analytical brains are out of the picture. While we're sleeping, our body and our mind are resting, but our soul is still awake. This gives God and the angels an opportunity to bypass our "hamster-wheel brain" that can't stop spinning, which is one of the biggest reasons the angels can't get their messages through to us. Our way-too-busy lives keep us from receiving the angelic inspiration that usually only comes in moments of calm and stillness. When I'm sleeping, my rational, thinking brain is on hold, and as a result I'm more open to discovering things I wouldn't realize when I'm awake.

Once we get past our busy brain, the next biggest hurdle for many people isn't interpreting their dreams—we'll get to that next!—but remembering them in the first place! Through my time studying the Language of Dreams and Visions, I've found a few handy hints that can help me remember my dreams come morning:

- Pray before you go to bed at night. Ask to remember your dreams and be intentional about remembering them. "Ask and ye shall receive" applies to all things, including dreams!

- Just as we are more apt to hear the voices of the angels upon waking, we are also more apt to see visions just as we are waking. Treat your time waking up as a sacred and special window for receiving angelic messages. Try to start the new day as peacefully as you can.

- A loud alarm clock can erase all memories of our dreams. I do wake up without an alarm clock most days, but that just means that I need to get to bed on time so I don't oversleep.

- Most importantly: keep a dream journal or voice recorder by your bed. Write down or record your dreams and visions as they occur or immediately upon waking. Daniel did this in the Old Testament:

In the first year of Belshazzar king of Babylon, Daniel had a dream, and visions passed through his mind as he was lying in bed. He wrote down the substance of his dream. (Daniel 7:1)

I prefer to jot my dreams and visions down as I receive them rather than waiting until morning. If I don't write them down immediately, I often forget what they were. When I write them down in the middle of the night, I don't turn a light on so I can fall back asleep more easily.

Once you have your dreams written down, you will need to discern them. We use our discernment anytime we interpret angelic messages—or any messages, for that matter!—as it helps us distill the most pertinent and applicable information. Discernment is the important ability of "translating" the Language of Dreams and Visions into messages you can easily understand. It is also one of the tricky parts about the Language of Dreams and Visions.

While there are some tools out there to help us discern our dreams and visions, keep in mind that you are your own best dream interpreter. Sometimes I find that people don't trust their own angel connection so they try to get others to interpret their dreams and visions for them. While a good friend might be able to help you discern your dream, *you* are the final authority. Don't abdicate your power. Use the method of discernment or interpretation that feels right to you in the moment for that particular dream and know that it may change for the next dream—that is A-OK! Additionally if the message you get from your friend, your book, etc., doesn't feel right, keep on looking until you find the interpretation that fits. You'll know the right message when you find it. Below are a few tools for discernment and good jumping-off points while you are still building your connection with your angels through dreams and visions.

Dream symbols books. Find a book that speaks to or resonates with you, as many dream symbols books are different. Ask to be shown which book is the right one for you. Currently I use one book by a Christian author and three by secular authors. In any dream book you will find definitions for dream symbols that don't feel exactly right to you. That's okay. That doesn't mean the whole book is wrong. Instead of tossing the whole book, look elsewhere for the definitions to the symbols that you're feeling iffy about because, as we've all learned, there's nothing wrong with a second opinion. You can also try researching your dream symbols online. Unfortunately I have yet to find an online dream dictionary that I'm comfortable with.

Remember that the angels will use symbols that are meaningful to you. If I were to see a tractor in my dream, it would make me happy because my dad worked at a tractor plant. The angels would probably be giving me a "hello" from him if they showed me a tractor, but for someone who grew up on a farm, a tractor might be a symbol of hard work. It might also be a symbol of something that makes life easier for them as opposed to a plow. To get to the core of your dreams, use your dream symbols book to look up the general definitions and supplement them with your personal feelings about the symbols in your dream.

Prayer. Go into a period of prayer and ask to be shown the meaning of your dream or vision. When I got my first dream symbols book, I asked God and the angels to use the symbols and the definitions in that book when they spoke to me in my dreams, so that we would all be on the same page and I would know I was using the right "key" to decode my dreams.

In prayer, ask God to send your angels to help you discern the dream or vision as in Daniel 8:16:

And I heard a man's voice from the Ulai calling, "Gabriel, tell this man the meaning of the vision."

Even those who experienced dreams and visions in the Bible asked God to help them understand the messages in their visions and dreams just as Gabriel was called to help Daniel discern his vision.

Emotions. Notice how you felt during the dream and when you woke. Peaceful? Anxious? Here's where the Language of Feelings and the Language of Dreams and Visions can merge. Your feelings will give you clues about the interpretation of your dreams. If you see a dream symbol that makes you feel comfortable, it's likely a sign you're on a steady, pleasant path. If you discern that a dream is a warning through a feeling of anxiety or fear, go into prayer mode to get clarification or to ask for further guidance on how to handle the situation.

For God does speak—now one way, now another—though no one perceives it. In a dream, in a vision of the night, when deep sleep falls on people as they slumber in their beds, he may speak in their ears and terrify them with warnings, to turn them from wrongdoing and keep them from pride, to preserve them from the pit, their lives from perishing by the sword.
(Job 33:14–18)

Recurring dreams. There are two reasons for repetitive dreams. The first is that it is an important dream about something coming to pass soon as in Genesis 41:32:

The reason the dream was given to Pharaoh in two forms is that the matter has been firmly decided by God, and God will do it soon.

The second reason for a recurring dream or vision is that you have not discerned it correctly or acted on it, as in my previous story about not resting once I had interpreted the angels' message. The angels are giving you a chance to reevaluate the dream and to come to the right conclusion—and to *act* on it as well!

Vivid dreams. Pay extra close attention if you notice that you are having dreams or visions that are more vivid than usual, as this points to God and the angels alerting you to the importance of that particular dream or vision.

Remember, just as with any messages that come through the angels, if you're not clear on what is meant or if you feel like you're not discerning the content correctly, you can always ask the angels to be more clear or to send the sign in a different manner that might be easier for you to understand. They want you to get the message and will do everything in their power to deliver it in a way that is comfortable and understandable for you.

The Language of Dreams and Visions might seem indecipherable or difficult at first because it requires so much interpretation and action on your part, but once you start remembering your dreams and investigating their meanings, you'll find that—just as in every part of our relationship with God and angels—it will become easier as you hone in on the correct messages that the angels are bringing you through your dreams.

Reflections

- When you say your nightly prayers, ask God and the angels to deliver messages to you through your dreams.

- Be intentional about remembering your dreams. Ask for God's help in remembering and keep a dream journal or recording device close to your bed to record your dreams as soon as you wake up.

- Use the dream discernment tools that resonate with you the most, and try out a variety of them to properly interpret your dreams.

- If you're still unclear, ask for further direction.

Prayer

Lord of the day and the night,

*Thank You for filling the Bible with dreams
and visions so that we can see another way
that You and Your angels speak to us.*

*Help us to remember our dreams, to
discern them correctly and to take
positive action based upon them.*

*For we ask all of this in Jesus' name.
Amen.*

Chapter 8

Improving the Connection: How to Help the Angels Help You

Be still, and know that I am God.

—Psalm 46:10

Now that you know what all the angel languages are, I want to share with you some ways to improve your connection with them. Whether you've never felt the presence of an angel or you've had many experiences with them, there are some things you can do to strengthen your angel connection. Please know that I have learned all of these things through years of connecting with angels. I didn't start out doing all—or any—of them! Like any skill, you have to practice, and these are just a few of the ways that I have practiced growing a deeper connection to my angels.

From the list below pick a place where you'd like to start and work on that specific habit for a few weeks before incorporating another so you can ease into the practices. Don't let yourself get overwhelmed by the many options! As you deepen your angel connection over the next few weeks, months, and years, you'll begin to see how these practices interweave and realize that it doesn't matter where you started; only that you *did*.

(A note to overachievers: Do *not* try to incorporate all of these ideas at once! It's not necessary. Again, just pick one, maybe two, and start from there.)

Slow down.

God intentionally gave us the Ten Commandments, and I'm pretty good with nine of them, but it's the Fourth Commandment to remember the Sabbath day that trips me up every week:

Remember the Sabbath day by keeping it holy. Six days you shall labor and do all your work, but the seventh day is a sabbath to the Lord your God. On it you shall not do any work, neither you, nor your son or daughter, nor your male or female servant, nor your animals, nor any foreigner residing in your towns. For in six days the Lord made the heavens and the earth, the sea, and all that is in them, but he rested on the seventh day. Therefore the Lord blessed the Sabbath day and made it holy. (Exodus 20: 8–11)

God devoted an entire day of the week to rest! He actually used more words explaining this commandment than any of the others. He clearly is giving us directions to rest. Let's listen to Him! I have found that my angel connection is stronger when I am well rested.

Remember, the voice of God and His angels can't get through to us if we're constantly racing around and have no moments for peace or reflection. As Dallas Willard said—as quoted by John Ortberg in his book *Soul Keeping*—"You must ruthlessly eliminate hurry from your life. . . . There is nothing else. Hurry is the great enemy of spiritual life in our day."

The opening verse for this chapter talks about our need to "be still." This is a foreign concept for many of us in the world today! But eliminating hurry from our life allows for moments of spaciousness and stillness, which in turn allow for space for the angels to connect with us—something they can't do if our attention is elsewhere. Remember to slow down and rest to allow more spaciousness for your angels to enter your life. You can't squeeze angelic communication in between work and little league; you need to let in moments of rest and quiet to expand your relationship with the angels. Natural pauses in the day were what allowed the figures in the Bible to communicate with angels more regularly than we do now—building these same pauses and rest moments into your day will bring the same result: a deeper intimacy with God and a better understanding of your angels and the messages they are communicating with you.

Spend time in silence.

The messages we receive from angels can be subtle and quiet. The Bible tells us that the voice of God is "still" and "small." Some versions of the Bible call His voice a "whisper" as in 1 Kings 19:12. Should we expect His angels to be any louder? When we silence ourselves, we can begin to receive their messages.

Mother Teresa was well acquainted with the still, small voice of God when she said, "God is the friend of silence. See how nature—trees, grass, grow in silence; see the stars, the moon and the sun, how they move in silence. . . . We need silence to be able to touch souls."

I spend two days in silence each month. They are set aside on my calendar, and I schedule my life around them. When I reenter the speaking world after my silent days, I am refreshed, renewed, and ready to face the new day. Try starting with ten minutes of silence each day—this can be when you're just waking up and journaling your dreams, right before bed after you say goodnight to your loved ones, or even during your lunch break when you can take a moment to sit by yourself, away from colleagues and phones, and allow a pause to reconnect with God through silence. There is an old saying, "If your mouth is moving, you're not listening." I think the same is true when it comes to our communication with the angels. When you step into silence, you give the angels an opportunity to speak and have a better chance of hearing the messages that they bring.

Take care of your physical body.

I'll be very honest with you: you can get some angel messages without taking good care of yourself. When I first learned about angels, my diet was horrible. Cookies, candy, and fudge were my main food groups. Through the years as I have progressed in my relationship with the angels, they have gradually encouraged me to let go of soy, gluten, and sugar. The angels guided me to give these items up for my own health, and I find that my angel connection is better when my body is happy, fed on good, nutritious food, and maintained through exercise. I believe this is a "put good in, get good out" situation where the angels have prescribed a diet for me that will best suit me in connecting with them.

We learn in the Bible that Daniel is a vegetarian in Daniel 1:11–14:

Daniel then said to the guard whom the chief official had appointed over Daniel, Hananiah, Mishael and Azariah, "Please test your servants for ten days: Give us nothing but vegetables to eat and water to drink. Then compare our appearance with that of the young men who eat the royal food, and treat your servants in accordance with what you see." So he agreed to this and tested them for ten days.

I'm definitely *not* saying that you *must* become a vegetarian to communicate with angels; I only ask that you become aware of how different foods affect you, then change your diet accordingly if you feel moved or encouraged by the angels to do so as it will likely improve your connection to them.

Spend time with Jesus.

I am the vine, you are the branches; he who
abides in Me and I in him, he bears much
fruit, for apart from Me you can do nothing.
—John 15:5, NASB

How much time do you spend with Jesus daily? Are you so busy doing things *for* Him that you forget to be *with* Him? I have known people (myself included) who have been so preoccupied with making sure that everything is perfect for Jesus, they forget to be *with* Jesus. Christmas and Easter seem to be big hang-ups on this one, as we want everything to look and feel *right* and can sometimes become so wrapped up in the "doing" of the holiday that we don't take time for the "observing" of the holiday.

———————

As Jesus and his disciples were on their way,
he came to a village where a woman named
Martha opened her home to him. She had a
sister called Mary, who sat at the Lord's feet
listening to what he said. But Martha was
distracted by all the preparations that had
to be made. She came to him and asked,
"Lord, don't you care that my sister has left
me to do the work by myself?
Tell her to help me!"

"Martha, Martha," the Lord answered,
"you are worried and upset about many things,
but few things are needed—or indeed only one.
Mary has chosen what is better, and it will
not be taken away from her."

The story of Mary and Martha in Luke 10:38–42 tells us what Jesus really wants. He wants us to abide with Him, to stay closely connected in the *long term*. Abiding with Jesus makes it much easier to connect with His angels as they are His voice and bring us messages in His name. When we spend time with Jesus, we increase our intimacy with Him, and we are able to build our connection but more importantly our trust. When we know that the angels are the messengers of God and Jesus and we have a deep personal connection to Jesus, it can feel like each angel message is a note of love and encouragement that comes directly from the son of God! Can you imagine receiving love letters from Jesus? This is exactly what happens each time you communicate with the angels!

Connect with like-minded souls.

Talk about angels and angel messages with others who are supportive. Reinforce each other on your path. While there are definitely people who will encourage you with your angel connection, there are others who will try to knock you down or be skeptical. Be careful what you share with those who do not understand what you're doing, and be discerning with whom you discuss this part of your life. Reach out to those you trust and who can help support you in your journey, particularly while you are first learning the angel languages. You can share your experiences and learn from them together. For instance, I love trading angel stories with my like-minded friends because they reveal to me signs that I otherwise would never have looked for. Once they mention them, it's easier for me to be on the lookout for another way that the angels might come to me, as they've done for my friends.

Stay grounded and in your body.

Sometimes when I help someone connect to their angels, I will be shown that their soul is floating above their body. This can happen when a person has been through a traumatic or frightful experience. It also may happen when someone is sick and their body doesn't feel good. While you may not be able to see this yourself, one clue to realizing that you or someone you are with is outside of their body is that you may feel that something is off—as though you're just going through the motions in life and not really accomplishing anything. There might be something you really need or want to do, but you're not making progress on it. You may feel like you're not able to truly connect with people, or you feel spacey. While there can be other reasons for these sensations, they can also be a clue that your soul is not firmly in your body.

Life is much harder if you're not in your body. The whole reason God gave us our bodies is to accomplish His work in the world! We are His hands, feet, eyes, and ears! We need to be fully functioning to accomplish His glory, and our soul needs to be firmly in our body to receive the directions His angels are bringing us. If you aren't in your body, you can't use any of the three angel languages of the senses—seeing, hearing, or feeling—so it is imperative to try to connect with your body as much as possible in order to perceive the signs that the angels are bringing you.

If you feel that you might not be fully in your body, try the following exercises to bring you back:

- Inhale for a count of four, and then exhale for a count of four. Then inhale for a count of five, and exhale for a count of five. Work your way up to six, seven, and finally, eight. Then work your way back down. Continue until a feeling of peace settles over you.

- Sit on the ground. Reconnect with the earth beneath you and its link to your body. If you can do this outside, it works even better.

- Breathe in slowly, saying "I am." As you exhale slowly, say "at peace." Continue this for a few minutes or until you feel centered and balanced.

Be present in each moment.

Similar to being in your body, you can't receive angelic signs if you aren't paying attention or if you are lost in thought or worried about the past or future. Sometimes we're not effective in life (and in connecting with our angels) because we're not fully present in the moment. Some part of us may be busy rehashing an argument we had with our spouse. Another part may be concerned about an upcoming meeting with our boss. Yet another part may be excited about a party we have planned. Don't be scattered. Focus all your attention upon the one thing you're currently doing.

Enjoy nature.

Go outside. Spend time in the garden. Hug a tree. Take a walk. Open your windows. God created the earth, and it was good! There is nothing more beautiful or that can more deeply strengthen your connection to God than seeing His hand at work in nature. Walk around barefoot feeling the grass under your feet and know that it was created by Him. Be grateful for the weather, the sky, the animals. Enjoy God's beautiful handiwork and sense your connection to Him grow deeper as you appreciate the world that He created for us.

Pray and meditate daily.

Set a regular time aside for God and the angels. Feed your soul first, and then go feed the world! By my prayer chair I keep my Bible, my rosary, and a notebook with a pen for journaling. I grew up Presbyterian and am now Methodist, but it feels good to hold my rosary when I pray. You might want to put a candle in your prayer area or a picture of Jesus. You'll know what is right for you.

Since God knows every thought we think, we could consider every one of our thoughts as a prayer. Taking a daily prayer and meditation time means that we are praying on purpose—not by accident. Purposeful prayer is powerful prayer. As previously discussed, prayer and meditation are also moments when we can still our hamster-wheel brain and make space for inviting the angels to speak to or through us. This is one of the most important daily practices to get into in order to strengthen your connection with the angels because it gives them a consistent opportunity to communicate with you when you are not distracted by something else.

Take action as guided by the angels.

Trust the little messages you get from your angels and take action on them, and bigger messages will come. As you begin to trust in the angels, yourself, and your relationship with them, start with baby steps toward what the angels are guiding you to do. As you build your relationship, you'll grow more and more comfortable with taking the steps the angels want you to take, which in turn will lead them to bring you more messages with more actions until it becomes a cycle of receiving divine messages and taking divinely guided action.

Ask and ye shall receive.

If there's something that you need, ask for it. Ask again. Then ask again. Through continually asking we strengthen ourselves and allow ourselves to surrender to God's will, knowing He will provide what is needed—even if it isn't always what we had in mind. Asking allows change to take place within us and prepares us to receive.

As I've said over and over again, the angels cannot come to you unless you ask them to, so part of asking for what you need is inviting the angels to help. It doesn't do you any good to say "Bring me more abundance" over and over—you are the one who will have to take action to get what you want. But God is always willing to provide. Try asking instead, "Please guide me in how I can achieve greater abundance in my life." Now you've invited them to bring you messages, knowing that you will need to act on the guidance you receive in order to make a change. Consider 2 Corinthians 12:8–10:

Three times I pleaded with the Lord to take it away from me. But he said to me, "My grace is sufficient for you, for my power is made perfect in weakness." Therefore I will boast all the more gladly about my weaknesses, so that Christ's power may rest on me. That is why, for Christ's sake, I delight in weaknesses, in insults, in hardships, in persecutions, in difficulties. For when I am weak, then I am strong.

Be creative.

Draw, play music, sing, dance, make art. I took an art class at a women's retreat many years ago. At the time, I hadn't done art in years, but I became so involved in the activities that I completely lost track of time. I connected with God in a very deep and powerful way. For some people art is a way to connect with God and the angels, so be willing to experiment with artistic expression of all kinds to see if any of them feel right for your personal connection with God.

One fun exercise is to take a blank canvas or paper along with paints or crayons or whatever tools you like. Invite the angels to create a picture with you, then draw or paint what they suggest. This kind of exercise is a fun way to deepen your connection and intimacy with the angels and a chance to practice digging into the languages of the angels to see how the messages come to you.

Don't compete.

When my best friend Christine heals others, her hands get really hot. When I heal others, my hands stay cold. I used to be really jealous of the physical effect that happened to her hands! Why didn't my hands get hot like hers did? The fact that her hands got hot made me think that her gift was affirmed while mine was not. However, when I see visions, they are very clear. I see details. When Christine has a vision, she only sees lights. She used to be jealous of me!

Don't compare your gifts to others. When you measure yourself by others, you will discount your own gifts and likely miss a great many messages simply because you don't believe your own gifts are valid—but they are! God created you the way He did so you can help with your unique gifts—not anyone else's. Your gifts are perfect for you and just what is needed on your particular path! Celebrate your gifts and the gifts of your friends. Be grateful we're all different! God doesn't need two of any of us!

Relax, don't strain.

Trying to *make* the angels bring you messages does not work. Forcing yourself to listen for angelic messages does not work. *Allowing* does work. Relax. Breathe. Let the angels gently bring you God's messages. As your connection to them grows, this process will become more and more easy and effortless.

Have fun.

As the old saying goes, "All work and no play makes Jack a dull boy." This is one thing I have to constantly remind myself of. I enjoy having fun, but I rarely set aside the time to do nothing other than *have fun*. Make room in your life for fun—not work, not multitasking, just fun! The Bible tells us it's good medicine for everything that ails you, as in Proverbs 17:22:

A cheerful heart is good medicine, but a crushed spirit dries up the bones.

Having fun will help you connect with your angels by putting you in a good space to receive their messages!

Say "thank you!"

Giving thanks puts us in a state of gratitude. Gratitude moves us closer to the angels. We are called to be thankful in 1 Thessalonians 5:18: *"Give thanks in all circumstances; for this is God's will for you in Christ Jesus."*

Whew! You made it! That was a long list. Remember: don't try to do all of these at once! Even starting with just one item on this list will move you closer to connecting with the angels. You can work on integrating more of them once you feel comfortable and moved to do so—your angels may even help you pick which part of the list to work on next!

Prayer

Lord God, Creator of the angels,

*I earnestly desire to connect
with Your Holy angels.*

*Show me how You want me to begin
increasing my angel connection.*

Help me to take the steps You guide me to take.

In Jesus' name. Amen.

Afterword

Guided by Angels in Difficult Times

Several years after my divorce the angels introduced me to Doug, and let me tell you, true love is a wonderful thing. We dated, fell in love, and married. He swore that he knew I was The One from the moment he laid his eyes on me. We built a small home together in the country. He understood my angel connection and encouraged it. I encouraged him to follow his dreams. We started a small business together. Life was full and grand.

A few years after we married the angels encouraged me to go back home to see my parents. They were both nearing ninety years old, and I didn't know how long I would have them around. The angels explained to me that I needed to help my father prepare for his transition to heaven. I didn't like that message but it felt true, so I bought the ticket. When I was home, I didn't mention anything about the angels' message to Dad, but somehow he knew. He wanted to make sure everything was in place for him to leave. At his direction, we discussed his preplanned funeral, double-checked his will, and made sure all the proper paperwork was prepared. I could see him relax as he realized everything had been done and my mom would be well taken care of. It was a tough trip for me, but I was grateful to be able to support my dad in this way.

When I got back home, everything returned to its usual bliss, until Doug got the big "C"—cancer. The diagnosis was acute myeloid leukemia or AML, an aggressive form of leukemia. His five-year chance of survival was 18 percent. The diagnosis rocked me to my core. During this time, Doug made choices about his health that I didn't agree with, but the angels made it clear that they were his to make. My job was to support him in his decisions.

Before Doug began treatment, our first step was to put together our Angel Team—or The A-Team, as I like to think of them! The team included friends of ours who agreed to pray for us and assist us when we needed help. It was wonderful to feel so supported and loved.

Doug's initial treatment meant an isolation room at the hospital for thirty days, in which he was to receive massive rounds of chemotherapy. Only scrubbed and gowned doctors and nurses could get in to see him. I had to talk to him on a phone through a window just like in prison movies.

I was on my way to visit him one day when my sister called to tell me Dad had passed away. Although the angels had given me signs to call Dad the day before, I had felt too tired from work and my trips to see Doug and had decided to wait a few days. Now it was only one day later, and it was too late. When I finally got to the hospital, I told Doug about Dad's transition through the glass window and phone system. Doug was brokenhearted. He truly loved my dad. They had a lot in common. We wanted to hug each other and cry together, but a pane of glass separated us. Doug obviously couldn't go to the funeral with me although he wanted to. He was so disappointed that he couldn't be there to support me.

I bought a plane ticket and flew home. My parents still went to the same church they had been members of for well over fifty years. It was lovely to be supported by this kind, familiar congregation. Most of them still remembered me from when I was a little girl.

On the way back from the funeral, exactly one month from the day Doug was diagnosed with leukemia, I got a phone call while I was changing planes. A friend told me I could not go home because a wildfire had started very close to our house, and our area had been evacuated. They had no idea if our house was still standing. With terror, I realized that our cat Sparkles was still in the house. The authorities would not let anyone behind the fire line—even to rescue our cat. The blaze was massive, and because of high winds it was growing quickly. I felt like my life was falling apart: first Doug's cancer, then Dad's transition to heaven, and now a wildfire.

On the surface life was tumultuous at best, but in reality I knew I was safely held in the hands of God and the angels. I could feel the angels moment by moment, guiding me, helping me, showing me what to do next. Their messages grounded me and kept me calm in this extreme chaos.

The fire spread rapidly and ultimately became the largest in recorded Texas history. It was over a month before it was officially declared out. After spending a week and a half living with a friend, I was finally allowed to return to our home. Our neighborhood looked like a war zone. I have never seen such devastation in my life; there are not words to adequately describe it. Everything was black or gray and charred. Empty. Desolate. Eerily silent. The beautiful, welcoming loblolly pines simply no longer existed. I was shocked to find that the two homes adjacent to ours had burned to the ground, and the fire had completely encircled our house. It burned bushes less than ten feet from the house . . . but it never touched our home. Even Sparkles, who had been stranded inside, was alive and well. We lost over three hundred trees and our home had smoke damage, but all I felt was relief at the fact that we still had our home, our lives, and our pet.

As Doug's treatment continued and our Angel Team continued their prayers of support, I continued to receive the angels' guidance. We were so appreciative for all the gifts that were arising from our angels (the human ones and the divine ones). Although so much chaos surrounded us, I remember feeling completely at peace and trusting in God's will. In fact, when one of my friends e-mailed me to check on things, this was my response:

Somehow through this whole process I have
felt and known the presence of the angels.
I have always known that we are perfectly
protected—even with all indications to the con-
trary. I cannot explain it, except that there is a
calmness that flows through me. I am so grate-
ful for it. I really am feeling blessed.

Blessed—that was exactly how I felt. In the midst of cancer, death, and a wildfire, in the middle of all this turmoil, I was at peace and full of gratitude.

Doug's thirty days in isolation were just the beginning of his treatment plan. Thankfully the rest was as an outpatient, so I got to be with him. Because of the combination of chemo and leukemia, his health slid downhill each month. It was devastating to watch my strong, vibrant husband become weaker almost daily. The angels kept supporting me. They told me what to ask his doctors and showed me ways I could support him. Then he got an infection that almost took his life.

It was Valentine's Day. The angels made it clear to me that I was supposed to enjoy my time with Doug, so that night we snuggled on the couch and watched a movie. After the movie I went to check my e-mails. As I was sitting at my desk, I heard a very quiet, "Oh no." Doug had just taken his temperature, and it was elevated. With decreased white blood cells from leukemia and the corresponding treatment, an infection could be devastating and had been our biggest fear all along. His elevated temperature was evidence of just the thing we didn't want. We drove to the emergency room where he was admitted to the hospital. I could see him fading, and when we got to his room, I saw his soul start to leave his body. I knew if it was his time that I should allow him to leave, but I didn't want him to go! I realized there was a very real chance that I would leave that hospital a widow. Miraculously, his soul reentered his body, and he started to perk up just a tiny bit. It was touch and go for a while, but six days later we left the hospital after a very close call.

Because of Doug's emergency hospitalization, the doctor decided to stop his chemo treatments. We had completed most of the protocol, and it was deemed too risky to continue. Although we had a difficult few months, Doug was officially declared in remission several months after that. We had a great celebration! Now life could get back to normal. We were so happy to put this behind us.

Doug began to gain a little strength, but then I could tell something else was off. He began to cling to me a little more, and there were times when the things he said to me just didn't make sense. He thought maybe it was chemo brain, but the angels told me it was something more.

One night I woke up and couldn't get back to sleep. Doug was by my side sleeping soundly. I got up and walked out of the bedroom. The house was silent. I was sitting by myself when I saw a light turn on in Doug's office. There was no one else in the house, so I couldn't figure out what had happened. I walked into his office and saw that for some unknown reason the light on his computer screen had kicked on. It was illuminating his empty chair.

It took my breath away. I knew immediately what it meant. Doug was going to transition to heaven, and that chair was going to be empty. "No!" I said silently. "No!"

I was angry with the angels for showing me this. What woman wants to know she is going to lose her husband? I said nothing to Doug about it. I silently hoped that I was wrong.

The next night when I went to bed, Doug was waiting for me. As I slipped between the sheets, he touched my shoulder, and I had an instant vision of the empty chair. As much as I wanted to be wrong, I knew without a doubt that Doug was on his way back home. I assumed that the leukemia would come back and take him. I had no idea what was coming.

I understood that the angels would only show this to me for my own benefit, but I still argued with them. This was not a path I wanted to journey down.

My dreams now included prayers, which was brand-new to me. In my dreams I found myself praying earnestly, "Thy will be done. Holy Spirit comfort me. Thy will be done." Another night I prayed, "Please take this cup from me. Yet not as I will, but as Thy will. Thy will be done. Thy will be done." I wasn't intentionally trying to pray in the middle of the night, let alone in words very similar to those Jesus prayed in the Garden of Gethsemane. These were the words that came into my dreams. The angels were preparing me for the road ahead. I couldn't see it yet, but I knew it was going to be very difficult.

The angels told me that Doug needed a CT scan of his brain. We went to two doctors, and they felt that the problem was that he was depressed. They both said that they would order a scan if he wanted one, but Doug chose not to pursue it. I was so frustrated.

A few days later Doug said, "Come snuggle me." I heard the angels whisper, "This will be the last time," but I didn't understand exactly what that meant. Because of their message I took the opportunity to thoroughly enjoy our time together. When we finished snuggling, I told Doug we needed to take him to the emergency room. I could just feel it. When we got there and the doctor came to see us, Doug began speaking gibberish. Finally I had a doctor that could see there was a problem. She ordered a CT scan, and this time Doug did not refuse.

The results of the scan showed a lemon-sized tumor in his brain, totally unrelated to his previous cancer. Surgery was recommended, but it was made clear that this was a fatal illness. The surgery would give him some extra time, but it would not cure him.

Now I found myself walking with the man I loved through the valley of the shadow of death. I ached for comfort for Doug and for myself. I wanted the green pastures and the still waters. I began to earnestly study Psalm 23, looking for comfort for us. I noticed something as Doug and I traveled through this health crisis together. Despite the chaos and grief around us, there were unexpected, inexplicable moments of absolute peace and contentment. Even though I didn't like what was happening, I could see it was my destiny to walk this wonderful man through his last time on earth. I wasn't happy that Doug was ill. I wasn't happy with his prognosis. Somehow though, in the process of this journey, I had surrendered to it, and there was complete peace in the surrendering.

I had the clear knowing that all was well—even though everything looked contrary to that. I felt a deep peace within me as I connected with God and the angels. Life wasn't giving me what I wanted, but somehow I knew that there was a bigger plan and purpose. I knew I was deeply loved and that love would carry me through everything that was to come.

The angels requested that I write things down. I was to journal about my prayers, what happened to me, what I thought, and how I felt. My friend Samantha told me that her angels said that my writing would be published and help many.

As requested by the angels, I began journaling about our experience. One of my prayer entries said:

> Today we find the perfect people to help us.
> Assistance effortlessly comes our way. People
> are happy to help, and they see what needs to
> be done. Support comes to us from everyone
> we meet. People are glad they have a chance to

*help. We bless them, and they bless us. Right
decisions are made. I support Doug. Together
we make the choices that serve us best. We are
loved and supported in all ways.*

My journaling continued:

*Our home is filled with peace. We are guided
through this stage of our lives beautifully and
peacefully. We feel joy in the time that we have.*

*Doug's crossing is a peaceful, easy, beautiful,
and loving process. I am guided each step of
the way. I know how to assist him. I enjoy
every moment we have together. My cup run-
neth over. We are blessed. We are loved.*

*Today is a beautiful day. I nurture and care for
myself. I relax. I love. I live, I breathe. I connect. I am One with All. I am guided. I hear
and follow the voice of the shepherd.*

On March 7, 2013, I walked my husband through
his final moments in his earthly body. I thanked him for
all he'd done for me and my kids. I told him I would
help his kids in any way I could. I thanked him for
loving me. I told him that I loved him and how much
I would miss him. And then God and the angels gently
took him home. It was peaceful, beautiful, and loving.

Doug made his transition over four years ago now,
and from this vantage point I can see the blessing of
the angels showing me that Doug would be leaving the

physical world, though I rebelled against it at the time. Because I knew what was coming, I was able to make every decision mindfully and purposefully. I got to write my part of the script exactly as I wanted it to be. I have no regrets, because I supported and loved Doug and let him play his cards the way he wanted to play them.

A few months later my daughter said to me, "Mom, if you were doing any better I'd think you were in denial." Similarly, my wonderful friend Lindsey, a hospice nurse, said, "I know it's not, but you make it look easy."

It hasn't been easy; in fact the hardest things that ever happened to me in my life happened to me during this eighteen-month period. However, this was *not* the hardest eighteen months of my life. Having the angel connection I now have enabled me to pass through this period much more easily than I would have otherwise.

In *The Power of Now*, Eckhart Tolle says, "When a loved one has just died, or you feel your own death approaching, you cannot be happy. It is impossible. But you CAN be at peace. There may be sadness and tears, but provided that you have relinquished resistance, underneath the sadness you will feel a deep serenity, a stillness, a sacred presence. This is the emanation of Being, this is inner peace, the good that has no opposite."

This peace is the "peace that passes understanding" that the Bible talks about. With the help of the angels it is possible for all of us to feel and know this peace regardless of what is happening in our lives.

There is not a person reading this book who does not have the ability to connect with their angels. Your angels are there for you. Be open to them. Know that they love you unconditionally.

Be sure to talk about and share your angel experiences. Allow others to share their angel experiences with you. Allow the mystical into your life through the power and love of God and the holy angels. Know that connecting with angels is not just a once-in-a-lifetime experience. Connect with them daily! Allow God to talk to you through His angels each moment of your life.

Jesus prayed for us to be "in the world, but not of the world." Learn to live with one foot firmly in the physical world and one foot in God's kingdom. This is much easier with the help of the angels.

I pray that each and every person who reads this book is blessed by God and His holy angels. Praise be to God! Amen.

Appendix A:
Messages from Angels
or the Holy Spirit?

A Note on a Few
Misconceptions about Angels

While discussion of the Holy Spirit mostly falls outside of the scope of this book, my fellow Christians often have trouble determining if a message is coming from an angel or the Holy Spirit. I've often asked—and been asked—if my experiences are truly coming from God, why does God bring me more messages through angels rather than coming to me through the Holy Spirit? My response is usually, "Why did God send an angel to Mary, Jesus, and many others in the Bible rather than coming to them Himself?" Like many Christians, I don't have an answer to these questions; but I do trust and believe that God knows what is best for everyone and that we will get our messages in whichever way God chooses, which often includes angel communications; therefore, it's to our benefit to be open to and understanding of the languages of the angels.

There's a simple way to think about the Holy Spirit versus angels conundrum: The Holy Spirit indwells—or lives as a presence within us—and angels do not. The angels exist outside of us, whereas the Holy Spirit is the presence of God within our being. The Holy Spirit is part of the triune God, and angels are not. In his book *Angels: Ringing Assurance that We Are Not Alone* Rev. Billy Graham states, "Both angels and the Holy Spirit are at work in our world to accomplish God's perfect will. Frankly, we may not always know the agent or means God is using—the Holy Spirit or the angels—when we discern God's hand at work. We can be sure, however, that there is no contradiction or competition between God the Holy Spirit and God's command of the angelic hosts." So in the end, when people ask me if their messages are coming from the Holy Spirit or from angels, I tell them that it doesn't really matter whether the message is from the Holy Spirit or from angels. The message will be identical no matter which of these two sources it comes from, as the message itself is guidance from God. These are just two separate means that He employs to communicate with us.

I've also heard people say that angels became less significant in scripture once the Holy Spirit arrived, and that's why we don't get messages directly from angels anymore. First of all, we most certainly *do* still receive messages from angels, but when I first heard this, I had to grab my Bible to investigate. It seemed somewhat logical to me that of course God would phase out angels once He had the Holy Spirit to deliver His messages—but I felt the angels calling me to research that statement.

What I found astounded me: The Holy Spirit arrives at Pentecost in the second chapter of Acts, but even after that there are five more angel visitations, just in the book of Acts alone!

Just consider Acts 8:26–29:

----

*Now an **angel** of the Lord said to Philip, "Go south to the road—the desert road—that goes down from Jerusalem to Gaza." So he started out, and on his way he met an Ethiopian eunuch, an important official in charge of all the treasury of the Kandake (which means "queen of the Ethiopians"). This man had gone to Jerusalem to worship, and on his way home was sitting in his chariot reading the Book of Isaiah the prophet. The **Spirit** told Philip, "Go to that chariot and stay near it."*
(Acts 8:26–29, emphasis added)

First, an *angel* gives the message to Philip, and then the *Holy Spirit* brings him a message. In these verses we clearly see angels working hand in hand *with* the Holy Spirit to bring about God's kingdom!

Not only do we see both angels and the Holy Spirit at work in the same person to deliver God's message in

Acts, but there's also further evidence that angels did not become less important because the words *angel* or *angels* are used in the New Testament sixty-eight times *more* than in the Old Testament. (That's 118 uses in the Old Testament versus 186 uses in the New Testament.)

Perhaps God not only wants us to flow with the Holy Spirit, but also to utilize the practical aspect of using angel messengers which our modern-day sensibilities have caused us to overlook. Wouldn't we, as Christ's body, be stronger and more connected if we used *all* of God's resources?

Another misconception I've heard about angels is that only *Christians* have access to angels. That is absolutely incorrect. The first time we find angels mentioned in the Bible is in Genesis 16:7 where an angel appears to Sarah's Egyptian maidservant Hagar. It's perfectly fitting that in the first reference in the Bible, the angel is helping someone who is not an Israelite—or a Christian! Angels are multicultural and nondenominational, and belief in angels spans across the religions of the world.

The last time the word *angel* is mentioned in the Bible is in Revelation 22:16. *"I, Jesus, have sent my angel to give you this testimony for the churches."* In this passage the word *you* in Greek is plural. *Jesus sent His angel to all of us!* This is how much He loves us! The significance of this statement is only compounded by the fact that these were the last words Jesus spoke in the Bible.

It's important for us to confront these misconceptions as these are some of the ideas that so often stand between people and their ability to reach out to the angels—they either believe that if the message is really important, the Holy Spirit will bring it; or that as a non-Christian that angels cannot appear to them, but that's entirely untrue. The wisdom of the angels is available for anyone who invites them into their lives.

Appendix B:
Discernment and the
One Scary Verse

*I am your servant; give me discernment that
I may understand your statutes.*

—Psalm 119:125

In 2 Corinthians 11:14 Paul states *"Satan himself masquerades as an angel of light."* This is one verse that I often hear quoted by people who don't believe that I am communicating with God's messengers or who are fearful of Satan's influence in these messages.

The important thing to note about this verse is that it actually is not about angels of light, it is about Satan. It doesn't say "angels of the light are all minions of Satan," of course! Nor is it saying that we shouldn't accept angelic guidance just because Satan may be speaking instead—what this verse is asking is that we use our common sense, discernment, and intimate knowledge of our personal relationships with our angels to determine what messages we're receiving.

Next, let us remember that the word *angel* is used about three hundred times in the Old and the New Testaments with positive connotations, so we need to be sure that we don't take this one verse and weigh it too heavily when there's also overwhelming evidence for the positive influence of angels throughout the Bible.

In Billy Graham's classic book *Angels: Ringing Assurance that We Are Not Alone,* he writes: "Ought not Christians, grasping the eternal dimension of life, become conscious of the sinless angelic powers who are for real, and who associate with God Himself and administer His works in our behalf? After all, references to the holy angels in the Bible far outnumber references to Satan and his subordinate demons."

Yes, there are fallen angels. Yes, there is a possibility that you could "see" them in the invisible realm. I also want to be clear that most people never do. The vast, vast majority of angel communication that I know of is all positive and from the angels of light. However, even for those extremely rare instances where you could encounter a negative force, the good news is there is an antidote to this, and it's already inside you: *spiritual discernment.*

Just as we used discernment to help us interpret the messages that come to us in the Language of Dreams and Visions, we can also use discernment in all of our angel communications and relationships. Discernment is what lets us choose what feels good and right for us, in our dreams or in the physical world. Discernment tells us when to trust another person in the physical world and also assists us in the invisible realm so that we remain safe and protected as we do God's work and His will.

I'll be honest with you. I argued with the angels about this portion of the book. I didn't want to include it. I much prefer to talk only about the loving angels, not Satan and his helpers, but the angels reminded me that it is essential to include these lessons because we need to understand and be aware of this realm without fearing it. That's so important. It's completely possible to be *aware* but not *afraid*.

Discerning Darkness

Discernment is like a muscle: the more you exercise it, the more it grows. As your personal relationships with your angels of light become more familiar to you, it will become easier and less frightening for you to discern where the messages you're receiving are coming from. For guidance on how to develop a discerning heart, we need look no further than the Bible. In 1 Kings 3:5–15 the Lord appears to Solomon and says, *"Ask for whatever you want me to give you."* Solomon gives a very interesting answer:

Solomon answered, "You have shown great kindness to your servant, my father David, because he was faithful to you and righteous and upright in

*heart. You have continued this great kindness
to him and have given him a son to sit on
his throne this very day.*

*"Now, Lord my God, you have made your
servant king in place of my father David. But
I am only a little child and do not know
how to carry out my duties.*

*"Your servant is here among the people you
have chosen, a great people, too numerous
to count or number.*

*"So give your servant a discerning heart to
govern your people and to distinguish between
right and wrong. For who is able to govern
this great people of yours?"*

*The Lord was pleased that Solomon had
asked for this.*

*So God said to him, "Since you have asked for
this and not for long life or wealth for yourself,
nor have asked for the death of your enemies but
for discernment in administering justice, I will do
what you have asked. I will give you a wise and
discerning heart, so that there will never have
been anyone like you, nor will there ever be.*

*"Moreover, I will give you what you have not
asked for—both wealth and honor—so that in
your lifetime you will have no equal among*

kings. And if you walk in obedience to me and
keep my decrees and commands as David your
father did, I will give you a long life."

Then Solomon awoke—and he realized it had
been a dream. He returned to Jerusalem, stood
before the ark of the Lord's covenant and sac-
rificed burnt offerings and fellowship offerings.
Then he gave a feast for all his court.

As the above story indicates, the first step to developing a discerning heart is to ask God's help. And look at the way that God responded to Solomon's request! The Bible tells us that God was pleased that Solomon asked for this and granted his request. It also goes on to say that without Solomon even asking, God also chose to give him riches, honor, and a long life, provided Solomon continued walking in God's way, because it pleased God very much to have Solomon request a discerning heart—so much so that he was rewarded in other ways as well.

It is important to note that Solomon requested a discerning heart, not a discerning mind. As we discussed early on, the door to the angelic kingdom opens through the heart, so we need to have discernment in our heart as well. "Discernment" in our brain is often just suspicion, which is not the same thing. Think of it this way: discernment is a door; we can open and close it to anyone or anything that we like at any time, and our opinions on whether to leave the door open or closed may change at any time. Suspicion is a steel barricade; it's possible for something to come through, but we're going to fight it every step of the way. Thus to have discernment in our hearts, we can determine what messages we want to receive—if any at all—as opposed to suspicion, which is a difficult barrier for our angels to break through.

While I didn't have the same profound experience as Solomon, recently I woke up from a dream with an equation for discernment that was given to me by the angels:

Awareness + Discernment = Right Action

In the middle of the night I was naturally a little tired, and I didn't understand how powerful this equation was until the next morning. I was struck by the wisdom of the angels once again. When we use the angel languages to become **aware** that something is happening in the world (the visible/physical world and the invisible/spiritual world) and we **discern** what's behind it, we will be guided to take the **right** action. For instance, if I become aware of a sign I have received—say one that tells me to quit my job—I would then take steps to discern where this message is coming from. Is it because I'm currently unhappy with my position or my coworkers? Is it because I'm starting to feel burned out? Or are the angels delivering me a message that I can't know all of the details for yet and I need to wait a while before I make a decision? When I am able to discern the meaning behind the sign I've been sent, then I can take the right action that the angels are guiding me toward, whatever that may be. In this example, if I discerned that this was a message from the angels and not just me having a rough day at work, I may feel moved to start putting more money into savings so I can take a three-month sabbatical while I look for work that I feel passionate about, or I may feel moved to immediately apply for new jobs and to get out of my current situation as quickly as possible. Discernment is like a combination of feeling and knowing, and when we have discerned something correctly, we will have a feeling of rightness—it's like when everything clicks into place. You may muddle over several interpretations of the signs you're receiving, but when you discern the message correctly, it will feel **right** as though a light was switched on inside of you.

As you move forward learning discernment, your experiences will look different than mine. We're all made differently so that should be expected. If I could give each of my readers a gift, it would be the gift of discernment. I wish I could give it to you, but it's something each of us must learn and develop on our own. I encourage you to eagerly desire it and to pray for it daily. God and the angels will give you many opportunities to practice your discernment, as they certainly do for me.

I've also included a prayer below that may be beneficial to you as you work on improving your discernment muscle. If you ever feel scared or doubtful, turn to this prayer, and know that God will gladly grant you the ability to discern whatever comes your way.

Prayer

Lord and giver of life.

I pray for the gift of discernment!

*I ask You to safely and lovingly help
me learn my discernment lessons.*

*Allow my angels to guide me and
keep me safe on this path.*

In Jesus' name. Amen.

Acknowledgments

Many thanks to Randy Davila who saw a book in me I didn't even know was there. Thanks to Allison McDaniel for skillfully guiding my manuscript into a readable book. Thanks also to Susan, Shirley, Anne, Suzanne, Danielle, Kelly, Michelle, and David for supporting and encouraging me along the way. A huge thank you to LIFE! Sunday School class and my Thursday night covenant prayer group for their prayers and support.

I am incredibly grateful to all the churches that have blessed, nurtured, and educated me through the years: Bethel United Presbyterian Church in Waterloo, Iowa; First Presbyterian Church in North Bend, Oregon; First United Methodist Church in Gurdon, Arkansas; Forest Hills Presbyterian Church in Grand Rapids, Michigan; Longview Community Church in Longview, Washington; Westlake United Methodist Church in Austin, Texas; First United Methodist Church in Pflugerville, Texas; First United Methodist Church in Bastrop, Texas; and Bethany United Methodist Church in Austin, Texas. Yes, I have moved a lot!

Thanks to my parents for loving each other and raising me in the Christian faith. *"Start children off on the way they should go, and even when they are old they will not turn from it."* (Proverbs 22:6)

Much love to Bridget and Micah. I'm so blessed to have you in my life!

I love you all.

About the Author

Kathy Mursch is an entrepreneur who grew up in a Christian family. Studying the Bible from a young age, she thought that angels were a lovely, esoteric, untouchable idea until she began receiving messages from them. Forced to face the reality that angels were indeed connecting with her, she begrudgingly began her own period of "research and development" into angels and how to connect with them. As she gradually opened to the angels, she found that her life became more balanced, meaningful, and peaceful.

Kathy has been actively helping others to find their own angel connection through workshops and classes for over eight years. She is a master teacher and educator with a fierce loyalty among her students. Her passion is speaking to groups and helping people find their own angel connection.

Visit www.kathymursch.com for more information and resources.